THE AUTHORS AND DOÑA MARIANA DE CORONEL

Carlyle Channing Davis (left) and William A. Alderson, the authors, listening to Doña Mariana de Coronel reciting her associations with Helen Hunt Jackson and facts attending the origin of "Ramona."

THE TRUE STORY OF "RAMONA"

ITS FACTS AND FICTIONS, INSPIRATION AND PURPOSE

BY

CARLYLE CHANNING DAVIS

Formerly Editor "Rocky Mountain News" and "Denver Times" and Proprietor and Editor of Leadville "Evening Chronicle" and "Herald Democrat,"

AND

WILLIAM A. ALDERSON

Of the Los Angeles Bar, Author of Legal Treatises on "Receivers" and "Judicial Writs," and "Here's to You," a Book of Sentiments

NEW YORK
DODGE PUBLISHING COMPANY
220 East 23d Street

CREDITS

The statements in this volume attributed to Susan Coolidge and Henry Sandham are from their contributions to Little, Brown & Co.'s illustrated edition of "Ramona," 1900.

"Glimpses of California and the Missions," from which extracts are used, was published in 1902 by Little, Brown & Co., and is beautifully illustrated by Mr. Henry Sandham.

AUTHORS' STATEMENT

IN this volume is related for the first time the true story of Helen Hunt Jackson's great American novel, "Ramona." The facts and fictions of the romance are distinctively designated, and its inspiration and purpose disclosed.

The originals of the characters of the novel are identified, and their true names given.

Innumerable fictions concerning the story that have gained currency, some having been commercialized by unscrupulous persons, are dispelled.

Many thrilling and heretofore unpublished facts pertinent to the romance and its author are here recited; some surpassing in tragedy the facts and fictions of the novel itself.

The illustrations have been carefully selected, and present scenes and persons inseparably associated with "Ramona," many having been especially produced for this volume, and others never before having been given to the public.

The contents of this book have been so prepared as to be interesting and intelligent to those who are not familiar with "Ramona," as well as to those who know the thrilling and pathetic California story.

Here are recited facts which constitute a complete story in themselves, and are, indeed, more thrilling and tragic than the fiction of the prevailing imaginary novelist.

Especially do we hope to create new interest in the greatest of American novels, " Ramona," and give tribute to its author, Helen Hunt Jackson.

CARLYLE CHANNING DAVIS
WILLIAM A. ALDERSON

Los Angeles.

TO

THE MEMORY OF

HELEN HUNT JACKSON

The Most Brilliant, Impetuous
and Thoroughly Individual Woman of
American Literature.

"What songs found voice upon those lips,
  What magic dwelt within the pen,
Whose music into silence slips,
  Whose spell lives not again!
O, sunset land! O, land of vine,
  And rose, and bay! In silence here
Let fall one little leaf of thine,
  With love, upon her bier."

CONTENTS

CONTENTS

CHAPTER XI

CHAPTER XII

CHAPTER XIII

CHAPTER XIV

CHAPTER XV

CHAPTER XVI

CHAPTER XVII

CHAPTER XVIII

CHAPTER XIX

ILLUSTRATIONS

The illustrations are made a special feature of this volume. Many of the photographs from which they were produced were taken expressly for the authors, and others have never before been given to the public. The publication of "Ramona" excited great interest in California, and several of the old photographers in the southern part of the State soon afterward visited and photographed many of the scenes mentioned and described in the story. These old plates were long since laid aside, and it was with great effort that they were discovered. As an incident to this labor, one photographer handled approximately four thousand plates in assisting the authors to select photographs for illustrating the text.

Where it is not otherwise stated, each illustration shows its particular scene as it appeared at the time "Ramona" was written. The two beautiful pictures of Don Antonio and Mariana de Coronel together, in Spanish apparel, show this couple to be just as Mrs. Jackson knew and described them. The posing was done under the supervision of Miss Annie B. Picher, Pasadena, California, soon after the publication of "Ramona," and the authors are indebted to her for the use of the plates.

INDEX TO ILLUSTRATIONS

HELEN HUNT JACKSON
(H. H.)

A TRIBUTE

CARLYLE CHANNING DAVIS

THE life of the author of "Ramona" might easily have been one long, gladsome summer day, the opposite of what to the world it ever seemed to be. Her earlier verse, as well as prose, may have reflected the sadness of younger years, but her Christian spirit and her artistic temperament finally enabled her to overcome a quite natural tendency to grieve over a fate none too kind, enabling her to enjoy to the full God's manifold blessings.

Left an orphan at twelve, bereft of her first husband after a decade of perfect wedded bliss, her only child taken from her two years later, and in the last fifteen months of her own life an almost helpless cripple, it is scarcely less than marvelous that she should ever wear that sweetest smile, that her eyes ever again should twinkle with the merriment they bespoke.

"I am astonished when I review my mercies,

and really feel as if all must have been arranged for my comfortable and respectable dying." Thus she wrote on her death-bed, from which also emanated some of the most cheerful verses ever credited to her pen.

The personality of Helen Hunt Jackson was unique and fascinating. She was born and reared within the town of Amherst, Massachusetts. Her parents were Calvinistic, possessed of but a narrow vision of the world and unalterable standards of right and wrong; of that old class of religionists who commence on Saturday to prepare a sour and serious mien for Sunday.

Her father was Nathan Wiley Fiske, professor of philosophy at Amherst College.

Helen was born with an irresistible and irrepressible passion for nature. From her earliest childhood she was wont to steal away to the silence and solitude of the woods and fields. She yielded to the call of the wild. She was adventurous and prone to exploration. Her sentiments were vivacious and enlivening. Her nature was sympathetic and pliable. She loved ardently, but she could hate with satanic earnestness.

She displayed a keen sense of humor. She was brilliantly witty. She was an iconoclast:

HELEN HUNT JACKSON

Taken in Los Angeles, 1884, a few months prior to her death.

HELEN HUNT JACKSON

From painting by A. F. Harmer, Los Angeles, 1883.

forms, ceremonies and customs were not laws to her.)

From her first husband she bore the name of Hunt. Her early *nom de plume* was "H. H."—Helen Hunt. Then from her second marriage came the added name of Jackson.

She was of the blonde type. Her eyes were gray. In stature she was small, gaining flesh in later years.

Her personality was irresistibly charming. She dressed daintily and neatly. Her attire, like her manners, had its individuality.

Colonel Higginson wrote of her: "To those who knew her best she was a person quite unique and utterly inexhaustible. She did not belong to a class, she left behind her no second, and neither memory nor fancy can restore her as she was, or fully reproduce, even for those who knew her best, that ardent and joyous personality."

At forty-two, after a decade of widowhood, she was driven to Colorado for relief from throat trouble, and took up her residence at Colorado Springs—"City of Eternal Sunshine"—destined to be her home to the end of her days. Colorado was good to her in every way. It gave to her renewed health. It provided a climate exactly adjusted to her requirements. It furnished an environment of mountain and plain and cañon that to her was a perennial delight. And it gave to her a husband, in the person of William Sharpless Jackson, ever congenial and worshipful, of whom any woman in the land might well feel proud. It also gave to her a home of inviting ease and luxury, the first real home the devoted woman ever had possessed.

Unfortunately these well-earned blessings came all too late. Mr. Jackson was a banker, financier, promoter, railway manager and man of affairs generally, with abundant longing for domestic enjoyment, yet with little leisure for its indulgence, while at the same time his talented consort, her soul stirred to its profoundest depths in the pursuit of a life's mission, was too much engrossed with its exactions to enjoy to the full, as otherwise she would have done, the comforts and the luxuries unlimited wealth provided in such lavishness.

Never before had Mrs. Jackson been free to spend money without considering the effect upon the domestic exchequer. Now her greatest enjoyment was in ministering to the sick and the afflicted, in providing for the wants of the needy, in relieving the ills of the unfortunate. This labor of love, together with her pen work, almost completely monopolized her time,)and left little leisure for what are known distinctively as social duties and pleasures.

Her most prized diversion consisted of walks and rides through the near-by cañons and over the mountains; Cheyenne Mountain ever preferred; it was a trifle more remote, not nearly so accessible, hence much more exclusive, than other local attractions, albeit less frequented; circumstances that doubtless lent added zest to her ofttimes solitary excursions.

It was to Cheyenne Mountain that Mrs. Jackson wrote this apotheosis:

" By easy slope to west as if it had
No thought, when first its soaring was begun,
Except to look devoutly to the sun.
It rises and has risen, until glad,
With light as with a garment, it is clad,
Each dawn, before the tardy plains have won
One ray; and after day has long been done
For us, the light doth cling reluctant,
Sad to leave its brow.
Beloved mountain, I
Thy worshiper as thou the sun's, each morn
My dawn, before the dawn, receive from thee;
And think, as thy rose-tinted peaks I see,

That thou wert great when Homer was not
born.
And ere thou change all human song shall die!"

A ranchman at the foot of the mountain, near Seven Falls, cared for a burro belonging to Mrs. Jackson, and one of the greatest of her privileges consisted in riding this sure-footed, faithful beast up and down the cañon upon a summer afternoon.

"Mrs. Jackson's Garden" is a name that yet attaches to a particular nook in Cheyenne Cañon, conspicuous for its wealth of wild flowers, which were especially dear to her.

Writing of Mrs. Jackson's domestic life at Colorado Springs, Susan Coolidge says: "It is not speaking too strongly to say that she reveled in it. Such a housekeeper as she grew to be is rarely seen. The spell of her enthusiasm affected her very servants. They were as much interested in her experiments and devices as herself, and even prouder of her successes. Colorado is a paradise for flower-lovers. From earliest spring to late autumn the ravines, the mountain sides and the mesas furnish a succession of delights.. The wide-eyed anemones, fair as those which star the Boboli Gardens, give place in turn to the stately pentstemons, purple, pink and scarlet, royal yuccas, and yellow columbines with spikes seven feet high, thickets of white and crimson roses, Mariposa lilies, painter's brush, its lips dyed with fire. There is no interval. It is like a procession from fairyland. Colonel Higginson, in his interesting paper on Mrs. Jackson, speaks of her as once welcoming a friend with more than twenty different vases of magnificent wild flowers, each vase filled with a great sheaf of a single species. I can well believe it. Her writing-desk and her picture frames were always wreathed with the kinnikinnick vine, of which she was so fond, and which in leaf and fruitage is like a glorified cranberry. Add a snapping fire of piñon logs for cold days, wolf and fox skins on the polished floors—all the gatherings of her life—little treasures brought from foreign countries, curious china, plaster casts, sketches and water-colors, many of them the gift of their artists, books innumerable, all combined and arranged with her inimitable gift of taste, and it is easy to imagine the charm of the effect. It was truly a delightful home. Her little dinners were particularly pleasant, and her devices for adorning her table as inexhaustible as original. I remember a wreath of pansies of all colors arranged in narrow tins half an inch high and curving in shape, so as to form a garland around the whole table, and her saying that it took exactly four hundred and sixty-three pansies to fill them."

I enjoyed the acquaintance of Mrs. Jackson during almost the entire period of her residence at Colorado Springs, though never a house guest, nor did I ever enjoy the privilege of protracted companionship with her. So highly prized was the privilege of acquaintance that no business or other consideration was ever permitted to interfere when opportunity offered for meeting her at her home or elsewhere; and such opportunities were quite frequent.

The acquaintance began in Colorado before her marriage to Mr. Jackson, and continued to the end. I met her at various times in Denver, Manitou and Colorado Springs, and at her ideal home in the latter city was a frequent visitor from about 1876 to the date of her death, although much of the time she was absent in New York, Washington and in Southern California, in pursuit of a mission that obsessed her.

The Indian question was ever uppermost in her mind, and it is questionable if any other topic introduced, upon the occasion of those

visits to her home, engaged her serious thought or attention.

Local conditions seemed to conspire against her, and in view of them it is not remarkable that Mrs. Jackson should have been deprived of the sympathy and support of her friends and neighbors. She was scarcely located in Colorado when the citizen soldiery of the capital was called out to defend it from anticipated attacks by the Arapahoes and Cheyennes. In 1879 occurred the Thornberg massacre, the murder of Agent Meeker and the capture of his wife and daughter by Chief Ouray's band of Utes, events that agitated the Territory and the State as nothing before or since has done.

Sympathy with her at the time was not to be expected; but interest in her work, and in the enthusiasm displayed in it, was simply impelling. She wouldn't let us talk about anything else. (Her relation of experiences among the Mission Indians of California was of thrilling interest, albeit comprehension of the import of it all was not easy.)

Of far greater concern to me was the announced purpose of Mrs. Jackson to tell the story in the form of a romance. This was in 1883, after her return from California. That at once appealed to my imagination, and I readily recalled the outline she gave of it when, a few years later, I came to Southern California and became acquainted with a number of its real characters.

My wife had for more than a year been a member of the household of the eldest son of the mistress of Camulos ranch—Ramona's home —Ex-State Senator R. F. del Valle, and well knew his mother, Doña Ysabel del Valle, his sister, Mrs. Josefa Forster, and two brothers, Ignacio and Ulpiano. She had, indeed, been present at the birth of Lucretia Louise del Valle, at this writing just returned with her distinguished father, Senator del Valle, from a mission of peace to the warring factions in Old Mexico, sent as the special representative of the Secretary of State, W. J. Bryan. She not only knew these personages most intimately, but had spent varying periods at Camulos ranch, and every scene there recalling Ramona and Alessandro was familiar to her. Doña Mariana de Coronel, the intimate friend of Mrs. Jackson, also was an old acquaintance. Hence my interest in "Ramona" became especially enlivened.

Unfortunately, I did not at the time share in Mrs. Jackson's sympathy for the Indian to any great extent, nor did I possess the clarity of vision essential to a correct understanding of the Indian question, as it presented itself to her. As stated in the body of this volume, Mrs. Jackson enjoyed something of a monopoly of her views, and was quite without a genuine sympathizer with her work in the entire State of Colorado. My ignorance of the real merits of the controversy was neither greater nor less than that entertained by the average citizen. Mrs. Jackson might turn on ever so many side-lights, yet the feeling in Colorado at the time was almost universal that the only good Indian was the dead Indian.

We had not read to full purpose "A Century of Dishonor"; we looked upon Ramona and Alessandro and Father Salvierderra as beautiful characters, but we didn't look toward Temecula. We only thought of the Arapahoes and Cheyennes stealing upon Denver in the silence of night, with murderous intent. We looked away from Pechanga. We harped upon Father Meeker; but we never permitted ourselves to dwell upon the atrocious outrages committed and being committed by the white man on the Indians all over the San Jacinto Mountains! Ignorance and cowardice and hate had made savages of the whites, and left Helen Hunt Jackson to fight the battle alone.

She died at San Francisco, August 12, 1885, in her fifty-fourth year.

Well may we marvel at her courage, her patience, her perseverance and her unyielding zeal. Well may we, with Susan Coolidge, wonder:

"What was she most like? Was she like the
    wind
Fresh always and untired, intent to find
  New fields to penetrate, new heights to gain;
Scattering all mists with sudden, radiant wing;
Stirring the languid pulses; quickening
  The apathetic mood, the weary brain?

Or was she like the sun, whose gift of cheer
Endureth for all seasons of the year,
  Alike in winter's cold or summer's heat?
Or like the sea, which brings its gifts from far,
And still, wherever want and straitness are,
  Lays down a sudden largess at their feet?

Or was she like a wood, where light and shade,
And sound and silence, mingle unafraid;
  Where mosses cluster, and, in coverts dark,
Shy blossoms court the brief and wandering air,

Mysteriously sweet; and here and there
  A firefly flashes like a sudden spark?

Or like a willful brook, which laughs and leaps
All unexpectedly, and never keeps
  The course predicted, as it seaward flows?
Or like a stream-fed river, brimming high?
Or like a fruit, where those who love descry
  A pungent charm no other flavor knows?

I cannot find her type; in her were blent
Each varied and each fortunate element
  Which could combine, with something all her own—
Sadness and mirthfulness, a chorded strain,
The tender heart, the keen and searching brain,
  The social zest, the power to live alone.

Comrade of comrades—giving man the slip
To seek in Nature truest comradeship,
  Tenacity and impulse ruled her fate,
This grasping firmly what that flashed to feel—
The velvet scabbard and the sword of steel,
  The gift to strongly love, to frankly hate!

Patience as strong as was her hopefulness;
A joy in living which grew never less
  As years went on and age grew gravely nigh;

Visions which pierced the veiling mists of pain,
And saw beyond the mortal shadows plain
  The eternal day dawn broadening in the sky;

The love of Doing, and the scorn of Done;
The playful fancy, which, like glinting sun,
  No chill could daunt, no loneliness could smother.
Upon her ardent pulse Death's chillness lies;
Closed the brave lips, the merry, questioning eyes.
  She was herself. There is not such another."

THE GRAVE OF HELEN HUNT JACKSON ON THE SLOPES OF CHEYENNE MOUNTAIN, COLORADO

DON ANTONIO DE CORONEL, IN NAVACANA SUIT, 1886

CHAPTER I

INSPIRATION OF "RAMONA"—THE CORONELS

THE devotion, vigor and perseverance with which Helen Hunt Jackson pursued her chief mission in life scarcely have a parallel. Her literary labor and fame culminated in the historical romance of "Ramona," the influence of which has been second to the production of but one other American purpose writer. The inspiration of "Uncle Tom's Cabin" and of "Ramona" was identical—the wrongs inflicted by a superior upon an inferior race. The chief aim of each was ultimately achieved; the one through immeasurable sacrifices of blood and treasure, the other through the peaceful evolution of public sentiment, leading up to a revolt of the national conscience, and compelling a reversal of public policies.

It is not an extravagant claim that the humanitarian impulse now giving direction to the conduct of Indian affairs by the Government had its genesis largely in the romantic novel "Ramona." The influence of the woman and her work was not only immediate but lasting.

It has come down to this day and hour. The tragedy of Temecula will never be repeated. The era of evictions has forever passed. The Mission Indians will not again be driven from their homes at the point of the bayonet. Helen Hunt Jackson's posthumous influence will continue to shield them.

On her death-bed Mrs. Jackson said: "I did not write 'Ramona'; it was written through me. My life-blood went into it—all I had thought, felt and suffered for five years on the Indian question."

Colorado, the home of the author of "Ramona," was long the border land. Its earlier citizens suffered greatly at the hands of the Indians. Many now living remember when even the capital of the State was menaced by roving bands of murderous Arapahoes and Cheyennes. The Meeker massacre is still fresh in the minds of its people. The treachery of the Utes may never be forgotten. But the prejudices of two generations, there and elsewhere, should give way to the fact that the Mission Indians of California belong to a different category: that they are peaceful, industrious and frugal; that they worship the white man's God, and endeavor, with a meager equipment, to raise themselves to his plane of civilization.

DON ANTONIO DE CORONEL

Intimate friend of Helen Hunt Jackson, and who, with his wife, gave Mrs. Jackson the material from which was written the story of "Ramona." "He is sixty-five years of age, but he is young, the best waltzer in Los Angeles * * * his eye keen, his blood fiery quick, his memory like a burning-glass." (Mrs. Jackson in "*Glimpses of California and the Missions.*")

Mariana W. de Coronel

Wife of Don Antonio de Coronel, the intimate friend of Mrs. Jackson.

Some of them loved their homes so well that they suffered death within them in stoic preference to going out into the world in search of others. Not a few so died as martyrs to boasted American civilization!

It was Helen Hunt Jackson's purpose to tell the whole pitiful story. It was her desire to paint it in its true colors in an appendix to her "A Century of Dishonor," but she was persuaded that it was the better plan to clothe it first in the presumably more attractive garb of romance, and then to follow with other works of a more historical character after the ear of the public should be secured. This was the sage advice of Don Antonio Francisco de Coronel and his wife Doña Mariana, living at Los Angeles; although these staunch friends did not begin to realize the enormous sale which the initial story was destined to reach, the far-reaching influence it was to exert.

In November, 1883, after her return from California to Colorado Springs, Mrs. Jackson wrote to her dear friends, Señor and Señora de Coronel: "I am going to write a novel, in which will be set forth some Indian experiences to move people's hearts. People will read a novel when they will not read serious books."

Nor does popular interest seem to decrease

with the lapse of time. The public library of Los Angeles now owns one hundred and five volumes of "Ramona," yet one can secure a copy only by means of a reservation and a long wait. It would seem that at least nine of every ten tourists read the story. Thousands of them visit the San Diego, the San Luis Rey, and the Santa Barbara Missions every season, confessedly because of the association with them of Ramona and Alessandro; and all esteem it a privilege to catch a glimpse of Camulos, as the trains of the Southern Pacific Railroad pass through the hallowed spot.

In the Coronel Collection at the Chamber of Commerce in Los Angeles is a portrait of Helen Hunt Jackson in oil, about 7 by 12, by Alexander F. Harmer; and beneath it is the little mahogany table on which Mrs. Jackson did much of her magazine work while in California. This table was made especially to her order, that she might write while in a reclining position, and under the personal supervision of Don Antonio de Coronel.

But the world, outside of Southern California, knows little of the Coronels, the relation of the author of "Ramona" to them, or the reason for displaying the portrait and the table with this particular collection of curios. Few indeed know that nearly all of the characters in the story were living persons idealized, that some of them are living to-day, or that the famous jewels, most unlikely incident of the plot, are still in the possession of the woman who most likely suggested to Mrs. Jackson the character of Ramona.

These facts and incidents constitute most interesting sidelights. The truth will be found to be, as so often it is, stranger than fiction. It is here first given, only once removed from the lips of the living actors.

CHAPTER II

MEETING THE CORONELS—BISHOP MORA—MRS. JACKSON'S AFFECTION FOR THE CORONELS

THE inception and development of "Ramona" is in itself a story of more than ordinary interest. It was the product of a peculiar and fortunate combination of circumstances and events, a happy mingling of realism and romance, the timely meeting of design with chance.

Helen Hunt Jackson came to Southern California in 1881, with a purpose not too well defined. She had been commissioned by the Century Company "to write something about the Mission Indians." It would have been an easy matter for her, and without leaving comfortable apartments in a hotel, to have prepared an interesting series of articles on the prolific theme, and her publishers would doubtless have been satisfied; but she was directed to higher and greater achievements by influences not reckoned with by her or those whom she represented. The inspiration may have been heaven-sent, but the instrumentalities that proved most potent were human, tangible, real.

The conditions were ripe for her mission; indeed, they were waiting for her. To the task of harvesting the matured fruit she brought a rare equipment. If events and circumstances were favorable, a less earnest, a less receptive, a less impressionable person might easily have failed to recognize their significance.

She brought a letter to Bishop Francisco Mora of the Los Angeles diocese. He gave her a cordial welcome and pointed the way. Don Antonio Francisco de Coronel, he assured her, was the traditional friend of the Indian in these parts, and to him and his noble wife she was sent with a suitable letter of introduction.

The Coronel rancho consisted of seventy-five acres of fruitful land lying in the valley of the Los Angeles River, on the southern outskirts of the city, and was covered with a noble growth of citrus and deciduous fruit trees. In the center of the tract was the hacienda, for decades a conspicuous landmark. It was a typical Spanish adobe house, with projecting tile roof and broad verandas opening upon the proverbial "court." It contained thirteen large rooms, more than sufficient for the needs of its two occupants, the old Don and his young wife; but Spanish hospitality took into account the necessity of providing accommodations for all comers, and it is not likely the hacienda was ever found to be too large.

The rancho was a gift to the Don's father from the Mexican government, in consideration of distinguished services in the field, the grant dating back to the early 30's. It descended to Don Antonio, who came upon the stage of action in time to be of service in opposing American aggression. He, indeed, had been singled out for the distinction of conveying to the Mexican capital the flags captured in various engagements with the invaders, nearly losing his life in carrying out his mission.

The rancho was still intact upon the occasion of Helen Hunt Jackson's first visit, 1881, but the subsequent growth of Los Angeles has completely obliterated all of the ancient boundary lines. Railroads cross and recross it, streets have been cut through, monster depots and factories built, residences erected and the once pastoral quiet of the locality has forever departed. The famous adobe dwelling itself, still retaining its original proportions, but fast going to decay, stands within the inclosure of a mammoth cracker factory near the corner of

Central Avenue and Seventh Street, and is now used for storing merchandise.

On her first visit to the historic hacienda amidst the orange trees, Mrs. Jackson met a cordial reception at the hands of Don Antonio and Doña Mariana, not because of her distinction or her worth, but because she bore a letter from the Bishop. They had never before heard the name of their guest. They had not been blessed with offspring, and had never read her "Bits of Talk" for young folks. They had felt the omnipotence of perfect, patient love, but not from reading her story of "Zeph." They knew, for it had come home to them as to few others, about "A Century of Dishonor," though they had never seen the book. They had been fighting the battles of the Indians for many years, in the most practical and helpful way, without the aid of allies beyond the mountains, without knowledge of the devoted work being done in other portions of the vineyard by the Helen Hunts and their colleagues elsewhere.

In the old and happy days of Church domination and priestly rule there had been no "Indian question." That came only after American "civilization" took from the red men their lands and gave them nothing in return. It ministered neither to their spiritual, intellectual nor physical needs. It neither helped them nor permitted them to help themselves. It simply abandoned them to their fate. In struggling with this they ever counted upon the sympathy, the advice and the material aid of Don Antonio and his tender-hearted wife, Mariana.

The situation had reached a critical stage when Helen Hunt Jackson appeared on the scene. The statement of her mission and the proffer of her assistance at once won the hearts of Don Antonio and Doña Mariana. The mutual confidence early established soon developed into friendship and ripened into love; and the last meeting of the trio was quite as pathetic as was the first. Doña Mariana was very ill, and believed she was on her death-bed. Helen Hunt Jackson had responded to a summons, and the speedy rally of the patient was doubtless largely due to her visit. "You are going to get well, Mariana," said Mrs. Jackson. "You will survive me. I feel that you will live to complete my work." Only a few weeks later Helen Hunt Jackson was among the blest.

A touching tribute to the affection between Mrs. Jackson and Señor de Coronel is her own statement in a letter from her at San Fran-

BISHOP FRANCISCO MORA, LOS ANGELES DIOCESE,

To whom Helen Hunt Jackson brought a letter of introduction and who introduced her to the Coronels.

"EL RECREO," OLD CORONEL HOME, LOS ANGELES.

Where Helen Hunt Jackson was ever a welcome guest, and where the story of "Ramona" had its origin. "A low adobe house, built after the ancient style. * * * I went for a few moments' call. I stayed three hours and left carrying with me bewildering treasures of pictures of the olden times." (Mrs. Jackson in "*Glimpses of California and the Missions.*")

cisco to Mr. Abbot Kinney, April 1, 1885, a short time before her death, describing her departure from Los Angeles a few days previous. "Nothing ever before so utterly upset me," she wrote. "Everybody cried that bade me good-by, I looked so ill. Even Miller, my driver, stood speechless before me in the car with his eyes full of tears! Dear old Mr. Coronel put his arms round me sighing: 'Excuse me, I must!' and embraced me in Spanish fashion with a half sob."

We quote from Mrs. Jackson's "Glimpses of California and the Missions" this description of Señora de Coronel and the Coronel hacienda: "In the western suburbs of Los Angeles is a low adobe house, built after the ancient style, on three sides of a square, surrounded by orchards, vineyards and orange groves, and looking out on an old-fashioned garden in which southernwood, rue, lavender, mint, marigolds and gilly flowers hold their own bravely, growing in straight and angular beds among the newer splendors of verbenas, roses, carnations, and geraniums. On two sides of the house runs a broad porch, where stand rows of geraniums and chrysanthemums, growing in odd-shaped earthen pots.

"Here may often be seen a beautiful young

Mexican woman, flitting about among the plants, or sporting with a superb Saint Bernard dog. Her clear olive skin, soft brown eyes, delicate sensitive nostrils, and broad smiling mouth, are all of the Spanish Madonna type; and when her low brow is bound, as is often her wont, by turban folds of soft brown or green gauze, her face becomes a picture indeed. She is the young wife of a gray-headed Mexican señor, of whom—by his own gracious permission—I shall speak by his familiar name, Don Antonio.

"Whoever has the fortune to pass as a friend across the threshold of this house finds himself transported, as by a miracle, into the life of a half-century ago. The rooms are ornamented with fans, shells, feather and wax flowers, pictures, saints' images, old laces, and stuffs, in the quaint gay Mexican fashion. On the day when I first saw them, they were brilliant with bloom. In every one of the deep window-seats stood a cone of bright flowers, its base made by large white datura blossoms, their creamy whorls all turned outward, making a superb decoration. I went for but a few moments' call. I stayed three hours, and left carrying with me bewildering treasures of pictures of the olden time."

CHAPTER III

FIRST MEETING WITH MISSION INDIANS—PREPARATIONS TO VISIT INDIAN SETTLEMENTS—CAMULOS RANCH—HOME OF RAMONA

AT her initial interview with the Coronels little more was accomplished than the establishment of confidence. A second conference was arranged for the following week. It happened to be Christmas day, 1881, a circumstance that appealed to Helen Hunt Jackson only after her arrival at the hacienda, so absorbed was she in other thoughts. Don Antonio, Doña Mariana and their guest were seated upon the broad veranda, the latter intent upon the details of her hosts' relation of Indian history and Indian wrongs, when the conversation was interrupted by the appearance in the yard of five mounted men, evidently in great mental perturbation.

"More trouble," quietly suggested the Don, accustomed to such visitations. "But it must be unusually serious, for these are all chiefs of their tribes, and their ponies indicate that they have been ridden a long distance and very fast.

Excuse me for a moment while I try to discover what it means."

The interview between the Don and the Indians was very animated, all talking at once. Mrs. Jackson soon became as excited as were the Indians. She could not understand their language, it being a mixture of Spanish with the tribal dialect; but their voices and manner indicated the deepest distress, and it was not difficult to perceive the import of their mission. It soon developed that the water rights to their lands, without which they were valueless, had been sold to a syndicate of white men; and these chiefs had come, as so often before, for counsel from Señor and Señora de Coronel.

On three distinct occasions had the life of Don Antonio been saved by the timely intercession of Mission Indians. The bond between them was indissoluble. The Don was their "padre," and Doña Mariana was in their sight little less than a saint.

Mrs. Jackson begged the privilege of talking with the chiefs, and, with the help of her friends in interpreting, she was soon established in their confidence. The inspiration at that moment seized her of visiting their villages, and the foundation was laid for securing, as she might in no other way, the fullest confirmation

MEETING OF THE MISSION INDIANS WITH DON ANTONIO DE CORONEL AT PALA MISSION, 1887

THE FAMOUS TORN ALTAR CLOTH, CAMULOS CHAPEL

"The white linen altar cloth, the cloth which the Señora Moreno had with her own hands made into one solid front of beautiful lace of the Mexican fashion * * * lay torn." "*Ramona.*"

of all that had been told her prior to their visit. This was most pleasing to Don Antonio and Doña Mariana, and the incident was regarded as fortunate; for Helen Hunt Jackson was assured of a welcome in the Indian settlements such as otherwise might not have been accorded her, and of knowledge that could be acquired by no other means.

The details of the journey were soon arranged. It included a long and wearisome ride over the mountains to the Indian settlements, with a side trip of observation to Camulos ranch, which the Coronels desired her to visit, that she might get a better idea of a typical Spanish abode, and because its occupants were not only zealous children of the Church, but traditional friends of the Indians as well. The Coronels assured Mrs. Jackson that Camulos ranch was one of the few remaining of the old Spanish homesteads where the original of a California hacienda still existed.

The "Century's" artist, the late Mr. Henry Sandham, and Mr. Abbot Kinney accompanied her on this journey. The owner and driver of the carriage in which they first rode was Mr. N. H. Mitchell, then conducting a livery stable at Anaheim, California, and now residing in Los Angeles.

It is not the purpose to follow Mrs. Jackson in her wanderings over the San Jacinto mountains. The details have been recorded in reports to the Government, published as an appendix to the second edition of "A Century of Dishonor." It is enough here to say that the name of Helen Hunt Jackson is to this day revered in the abode of every Mission Indian, and that, were it in the power of these grateful people, it would long ago have been placed in the Church calendar of saints.

Judged by the accuracy of her description of Camulos, it is likely the pictures she drew of Indian life were faithful and conscientious. She was at the ranch but a few hours, a circumstance which makes her portrayal of it all the more remarkable. In the short time she not only observed every detail of situation and environment, but while there evolved the chief incidents of the story.

"It was sheep-shearing time in Southern California." The Indians from over the mountains were there. All of the preparations described in the opening chapters of "Ramona" had been made. Father Salvierderra had come down from the Santa Barbara Mission. The matin songs had echoed through the court. Mass had been said in the little chapel in the orange grove. The altar cloth, made originally from Doña Ysabel del Valle's wedding gown, was spotless in its whiteness; but to the discerning eye disclosed a patch; for Helen Hunt Jackson saw it, and every visitor there since has seen it, although it is probable that on that particular day its existence was unknown even to Señora del Valle, the widowed mistress of Camulos. That dear, sweet soul, had been occupied with manifold household duties, and may not have been as observant of the smaller details as was her guest. However that may be, the patch was an inspiration, and provided the material for one of the most touching incidents of the story.

The dimensions of the ranch have since been somewhat curtailed, from forty-five thousand to nineteen hundred acres; but the ranch-house, or hacienda, with its picturesque environment and now historical belongings, survives the thirty years that have since elapsed, without essential modification or change. The visitor of to-day, stepping from a Southern Pacific train into the precincts of Camulos, will need to go through the yard where the shearing was done, past the shed in which the wool was stored and in the heat by which Felipe was overcome, to reach the entrance of the house; for the railroad track is in the rear of it.

Once within the court every scene will seem familiar; the arbor and the fountain and the chapel; the path leading down to the stream where Ramona washed the stains from the altar cloth, and where Alessandro first beheld the wondrous beauty of the maiden; the porch on which the raw-hide bed stood with its precious burden, and where the lover drew symphonies from the violin fetched at such cost of effort by José from Temecula for the delectation of Felipe, the invalid.

With the physical conditions unchanged in any material particular, it is not difficult to fancy the actual scenes being re-enacted. All of the influences of earth and air, of sheen and shadow, of restless foliage, and laughing waters of fountain and stream, combine to produce a state of consciousness, the disturbance of which comes necessarily in the nature of a shock.

CHAPTER IV

THE REAL RAMONA AND OTHER CHARACTERS — ALESSANDRO — GUADALUPE — THE RAMONA JEWELS—KILLING OF ALESSANDRO—THE ALESSANDRO-RAMONA ROMANCE

VARIOUS considerations, now no longer potent, have prompted the suppression of the real facts regarding the story of "Ramona" and the principal characters in it, and there have been circulated innumerable fictions.

Most absurd of the stories with which tourists are regaled is the one that credits the author with having been bribed to write it by interested parties for political effect, and that the $10,000 thus earned were used in setting up her husband in business. An equally absurd yarn that has found believers of a certain class, credited the authorship of the story to an unfrocked priest, whose nearly completed manuscript was appropriated by Helen Hunt Jackson. A brochure that originated in Los Angeles, and which has reached a large sale, contains a halftone from a photograph of an Indian woman living near San Jacinto, which the author claims is "the real Ramona." There is scarcely a settlement south of the Tehachapi that is not pointed out to the traveler as the "home of Ramona." She was married at every mission from San Diego to San Luis Obispo, if one but credits local legend. The real facts, until now withheld, are related within these pages.

For the Señora Moreno of the story there was doubtless a hint in the equally strong, but infinitely more lovely, real character who was until 1905 the queen of Camulos ranch—Doña Ysabel del Valle, for many years a widow. The property descended to her husband from his father, to whom it was granted before American occupation, for meritorious service in the Mexican army.

Ex-State Senator Reginald F. del Valle, the eldest son of the widowed mistress of Camulos ranch, may have suggested to the novelist the Felipe of the story. He has long been an honored citizen of Los Angeles, a prominent member of the local bar, and influential in the councils of the Democratic organization in California.

Ramona was a creation of Helen Hunt Jackson. She is supposed to have been a happy blending of two characters of the del Valle

CARRIAGE USED BY HELEN HUNT JACKSON

The carriage in which Helen Hunt Jackson commenced and made a part of her journey in Southern California. The gentleman in the picture is Mr N H Mitchell, who owned and drove the carriage.

BLANCA YNDART

As a child at Camulos, now Mrs. James McGuire, Los Angeles. "The one human document who may in truth be regarded as 'Ramona' of the story" *Page 35.*

household—Blanca Yndart, a Spanish girl, a ward of Señora del Valle, and Guadalupe, an Indian girl, given to the Señora when a child by a Piru chief. Blanca was the only child of U. Yndart, a resident of Santa Barbara. Her mother, dying when the child was five years of age, committed her to the keeping of Señora del Valle, and she lived at Camulos ranch as one of the family until she was fourteen. Then her father took a second wife, and Blanca returned to the parental roof, living there until her marriage, four years later, to James Maguire. Upon the death of her husband, some years ago, Blanca, with her two children, removed to Los Angeles, where she now resides.

Blanca is the one human document who may in truth be regarded as the Ramona of the story. She is of the purest Spanish blood, both father and mother having been born in Castile; and at sixty is still a woman of exceptional beauty. Her grandfather, Captain Yndart, was a seafaring man, more or less familiar with all the navigable waters of the globe. In his world wanderings, covering a period of forty years, he accumulated a chest of treasures of surpassing beauty and worth; and these are the "Ramona jewels." For years they were held in trust by Señora del Valle for Blanca Yndart, when she should be married; and they are still in the possession of Mrs. Maguire. They consist, in the main, of a large cross of pearls of rare purity and unusual size, a rosary of pearls, and a single pearl, pear-shaped, of extraordinary dimensions, and valued at several thousand dollars; "tray after tray of jewels," an East Indian shawl of texture so delicate that it can be drawn through an ordinary finger-ring; a number of dainty kerchiefs, and other rich and costly fabrics from the Orient—"shawls and ribosos of damask, laces, gowns of satin, of velvet."

A daughter of Captain Yndart, who subsequently married a cousin of the same name, was living at Santa Barbara when the old sea captain paid his last visit to the Pacific coast. Having a presentiment that he would not survive another voyage, he left the chest of treasures with his daughter, with instructions as to their disposition at his death. They were to be divided between his two grandchildren, Blanca and Pancho Yndart, the latter a cousin of the former. Blanca's mother was delicate, and realizing that she would not live to see her daughter married, she provided that, at her death, Blanca should be taken into the del Valle family at Camulos; Doña Ysabel del Valle being her nearest and dearest friend.

Mrs. Yndart, unwilling to trust others with the jewels, herself took them to the ranch, and it is said that not even her own husband knew of their existence. This was before the era of railroads at Santa Barbara, and the route chosen along the beach was safe enough when the tide was out, but a miscalculation was made, and in rounding a promontory between Ventura and the Malibu ranch, in water reaching almost to the seat of the vehicle, Mrs. Yndart and the treasures narrowly escaped being washed into the sea.

Upon the death of her mother Blanca went to Camulos and remained there for nine years, wholly unconscious of the existence of the jewels, or that such a rich marriage dot awaited her. This was strictly in accord with the wishes of her mother, which were sacredly respected by Señora del Valle. For thirteen years, and until Blanca's wedding, the jewels remained in a stout chest beneath the bed of the Señora, unseen by others.

Helen Hunt Jackson never saw Blanca or the jewels, but received the story from the lips of Doña Mariana de Coronel. The little Indian girl, Guadalupe, ward of Señora del Valle, was at Camulos when Mrs. Jackson visited there. She learned from members of the household of the relations of the child to Blanca, corresponding with those of Margarita to Ramona in the romance. The story of the girl had also been told to Helen Hunt Jackson by Doña Mariana de Coronel. There is a sequel to it which Mrs. Jackson never heard. It is an interesting bit of the tragedy of life, and is here related.

Notwithstanding their lineage and the traditions connecting them with Mexican rule, the del Valles have never, since American occupation, been wanting in loyalty to the United States Government. There have been numerous occasions for the visit of regular army officers to various points in Southern California, and in passing up and down the coast it was the good fortune of many of them to enjoy the hospitality of Camulos ranch. They were always sure of a cordial welcome there, especially at the hands of the elder del Valle, who, in his declining years, took special delight in recounting with those military gentlemen the thrilling events that had transpired in this borderland.

Upon the occasion of a visit of Captain Ridley, of the 4th U. S. Cavalry, to the ranch, he was struck by the singular beauty of the little Indian girl, whom he saw flitting in and out of the court. Turning to a companion, a citizen of Los Angeles who had accompanied him

HOME OF RAMONA

"Camulos dwelling, south veranda, as it appeared when "Ramona" was written. "The house was ... with a wide veranda on the three sides of the inner court, and a still broader one across

THE WILLOWS AT CAMULOS

Here were the washing stones and where Alessandro first saw Ramona, as they appeared at time of Mrs. Jackson's visit. "It had been more than once that he had found Ramona at the willows. * * * It was a pleasant spot—cool and shady

on this journey, he inquired with some agitation: "Who is that girl? She is the exact image of my sister!" His friend could only say that she was an Indian, given to the family by a Piru chief, but adding that the hostess would doubtless tell him all that was known of her.

An interview with Doña Ysabel del Valle was immediately sought, followed by a talk with the girl and a brief explanation; and when the officer left Camulos he took with him to his post, in Arizona, the child who bore such a striking family resemblance. She was his daughter! The child had known no mother save the kind Señora del Valle, and the parting with her was of course painful. Her own mother, an Indian woman, had been lost sight of in the wanderings of her tribe.

The circumstances under which this Indian girl, Guadalupe, came into the possession of Señora del Valle have been related to the authors by Senator R. F. del Valle and are these. Señora del Valle and others of her household were crossing the Santa Clara River, which runs through Camulos ranch; the Senator, then a mere youth, riding on a pony ahead of the others. He came upon a little Indian girl, almost naked, who was hiding in the bushes.

But when the Señora came up, the child brightened and ran to her, crying and pleading to go with her. The child had previously been at Camulos ranch and had been so tenderly and considerately treated by the Señora that she wanted to go to her, and had slipped away from her squalid Indian quarters, not far from the del Valle abode, and was on her way there. The Señora took the child to her home, and afterward the Piru chief, to whose tribe the child belonged, consented that she might become the ward of Señora del Valle.

The sagacity of the advice of the Coronels to Helen Hunt Jackson to visit Camulos is thus shown to have been happily vindicated. When she undertook to write "Ramona" it was only necessary to gather the tangled threads of fact into her loom as warp, and, with the aid of her fancy as woof, to weave the beautiful and symmetrical narrative that has done so much to enrich and elevate American literature.

There was no Ramona, and there was no Alessandro, in the relation in which they are portrayed by Mrs. Jackson. And yet there was a strong suggestion of both the incidents and the persons in events transpiring at the time. It is an historical fact that in October, 1877, Juan Diego, a Cahuilla Indian, was shot and killed by Sam Temple for alleged horse stealing, in the Cahuilla Range, a spur of the San Jacinto Mountains. The tragedy was not only known to Mrs. Jackson, but she made it a special feature of one of her reports to the Department of the Interior, and it is related in the appendix to " A Century of Dishonor." It is here given as written by Mrs. Jackson:

" An incident that had occurred on the boundaries of the Cahuilla Reservation, a few weeks before our arrival there, is of importance as illustrative of the need of some legal protection for the Indians in Southern California. A Cahuilla Indian named Juan Diego had built for himself a house and cultivated a small patch of ground on a high mountain ledge a few miles north of the village. Here he lived alone with wife and baby. He had for some years been what Indians called 'locoed'; at times crazy, never dangerous, but yet certainly insane for longer or shorter periods. His condition was known to the agent, who told us he feared he would be obliged to shut Juan up unless he got better. It was also well known throughout the neighboring country, as we found on repeated inquiry.

" Everybody knew Juan was locoed (a crazy condition affecting animals from eating a certain loco weed.) He came home at night riding a strange horse. His wife exclaimed: 'Why, whose horse is that?' Juan looked at the horse and replied confusedly, 'Where is my horse, then?' The woman, much frightened, then said: 'You must take that horse right back. They will say you stole it!' Juan said he would as soon as he had rested; then threw himself down and fell asleep.

"From this sleep he was awakened by the barking of the dogs, and ran out of the house to see what it meant. The woman followed, and was the only witness of what then occurred. A white man named Temple, the owner of the horse which Juan had ridden home, rode up, and on seeing Juan poured out a volley of oaths, leveled his gun and shot him dead. After Juan had fallen on the ground, Temple rode near and fired three more shots into the body, one in the forehead, one in the cheek and one in the wrist; the woman looking on. He then took his horse, which was standing in front of the house, and rode away.

"The woman, with the baby on her back, ran to the Cahuilla village and told what had happened. This was in the night. At dawn the Indians went over to the place, brought the murdered man's body to the village and buried

INNER COURT, CAMULOS, AS IT APPEARED AT TIME OF MRS. JACKSON'S VISIT

THE KITCHEN AT CAMULOS,

As it appeared at time of Mrs. Jackson's visit. "Juan * * * walked toward the sunny veranda of the south side of the kitchen, * * * where it had been for twenty odd years his habit to sit * * * and smoke his pipe." "*Ramona.*"

it. The excitement was intense. The teacher, in giving an account of the affair, said that for a few days she feared she would have to close the school and leave the village.

"The murderer went to the nearest justice of the peace and gave himself up, saying he had in self-defense killed an Indian. He swore that the Indian ran toward him with a knife. A jury of twelve men was summoned, who visited the spot, listened to Temple's story, pronounced him guiltless, and the justice so decided. The woman's testimony was not taken. It would have been worthless if it had been, so far as influencing that jury's minds was concerned. Her statement was positive that Juan had no knife, nor weapon of any kind; that he sprang up from his sleep and ran out hastily to see what had happened, and was shot almost as soon as he had crossed the threshold of the door.

"The Agent in San Diego, on being informed by us of the facts in the case, reluctantly admitted that there would be no use whatever in bringing a white man to trial for the murder of an Indian under such circumstances, with only Indian testimony to convict him. This was corroborated, and the general animus of public feeling was vividly illustrated to us by a conversation we had later with one of the jurors in the case, a fine, open-hearted, manly young fellow, far superior in education and social standing to the average Southern California ranchman. He not only justified Temple's killing of the Indian, but said he would have done the same thing himself. 'I don't care whether the Indian had a knife or not,' he said; 'that didn't cut any figure in the case at all, the way I looked at it. Any man that would take a horse of mine and ride him up that mountain trail, I'd shoot him whenever I found him. Stockmen have just got to protect themselves in this country.'

"The fact that the Indian had left his own horse, a well known one, in the corral from which he had taken Temple's, that he had ridden the straight trail to his own door and left the horse in front of it, thus tracked and caught, as he would have been, weighed nothing in this young man's mind. He was finally forced to say, however: 'Well, I'll agree that Temple was to blame for firing into him after he was dead. That was mean, I'll allow.' "

This is the real tragedy that gave to Mrs. Jackson the pictured killing of Alessandro in the Cahuilla range of the San Jacinto Mountains, where he, with Ramona, sought refuge from the trespassing white man.

The slayer of Juan Diego was Sam Temple, the brutal Jim Farrar of " Ramona." He continued to live at the foot of the mountain, more or less shunned by his neighbors because of the still popular belief that his victim was in the deplorable mental condition described by Helen Hunt Jackson, when, as Alessandro, he was found in possession of the white man's horse.

There was also current at the time a legend connecting one Ramon Corralez with a romantic elopement with a half-breed Indian girl named Lugarda Sandoval. The young couple in their flight are supposed to have experienced many of the painful episodes credited to Ramona and Alessandro in the night journeys over the mountains to San Diego.

At the same time Los Angeles was ringing with the sensational infatuation of a beautiful American girl of the city with a Saboba Indian, whom she met during an outing with her parents in the San Jacinto Mountains. They were not permitted to marry and did not elope; but it is likely the incident, in connection with the Corralez-Sandoval affair, furnished the inspiration for the Ramona-Alessandro romance.

CHAPTER V

WHERE "RAMONA" WAS WRITTEN—THE NAME "RAMONA"—HELPING THE MISSION INDIANS—MRS. JACKSON'S DEATH—LOVE OF THE INDIANS FOR HER

MRS. JACKSON returned to Colorado from California in the early summer of 1883. From her home on November 8th of that year she wrote to the Coronels, a part of the letter reading: "I am going to write a novel, in which will be set forth some Indian experiences in a way to move people's hearts. . . . The thing I want most in the way of help from you is this: I would like an account, written in as much detail as you remember of the time when you, dear Mr. Coronel, went to Temecula and marked off the boundaries of the Indians' land there . . . and I have written to Father Ubach and to Mr. Morse of San Diego for other reminiscences. You and they are the only persons to whom I have spoken of my purpose of writing the novel, and I do not wish anything said about it. I shall keep it a secret until the book is done. . . . I wish I

VERANDA ON INNER COURT, CAMULOS

"These verandas were supplementary rooms to the house." "*Ramona*."

SOUTH VERANDA, CAMULOS DWELLING

The raised part of south veranda, Camulos dwelling as it appeared when "Ramona" was written. Here Felipe was nursed back to health on the rawhide bed made for him by Alessandro.

had had this plan in my mind last year when I was in Los Angeles. I would have taken notes of many interesting things you told me. But it is only recently, since writing out for our report the full accounts of the different bands of Indians there, that I have felt that I dared undertake the writing of a long story."

This epistolary statement is used by many, and with evident justification, on which to base the assertion that Mrs. Jackson did not even conceive the story of "Ramona" while in California.

It is to be conceded that the novel was completed in New York. Señora de Coronel declares positively that Mrs. Jackson talked to her about the story, expressed a desire to locate the scene at the Coronel hacienda and told her she would name the novel "Ramona," all before her departure for the East in 1883.

Mr. Henry Sandham, the "Century's" artist, has declared: "At the time of the California sojourn I knew neither the name nor the exact details of the proposed book; but I did know that the general plan was a defense of the Mission Indians, together with a plea for the preservation of the Mission buildings, and so on; the whole to be enveloped in the mystery and poetry of romance. I had thus sufficient knowledge of the spirit of the text to work with keener zest upon the sketches for the illustrations; sketches, which, it may be of interest to know, were always made on the spot with Mrs. Jackson close at hand, suggesting emphasis to this object or prominence to that, as it was to have special mention in the book."

To the authors Señora de Coronel has declared that at her home Mrs. Jackson even selected the name "Ramona" for her intended romance, and relates this incident: "On a visit of Mrs. Jackson to the home of Dr. J. De Barth Shorb, near Pasadena, a child of the family was addressed as 'Ramona.' The liquid sound caught Mrs. Jackson's ear, and she remarked: 'That is a pretty name. Please say it again.' On her way home she continually repeated the name, evidencing she was impressed by its rhythmic sound. At my first meeting with Mrs. Jackson thereafter she exclaimed: 'Oh, I have heard such a beautiful name, Ramona, and I am going to use it as the title of my book.'"

Señora de Coronel says that Mrs. Jackson imposed secrecy on her and her husband concerning her intended romance.

It is not impossible to reconcile the quota-

DOÑA MARIANA DE CORONEL IN HER NEW HOME,
LOS ANGELES, 1889

RAMONA LUBO, CAHUILLA INDIAN,

Wife of Juan Diego, killed by Jim Farrar of "Ramona," at her husband's grave. Because Mrs. Jackson pictured the tragic death of Alessandro with the same conditions attending the killing of Juan Diego, this Indian woman has been erroneously proclaimed and commercialized as the "Real Ramona."

tion from Mrs. Jackson's letter of November 8, 1883, with the assertions of Señora de Coronel and Mr. Sandham. Mrs. Jackson came to California primarily as the special representative of the "Century Magazine," to secure information concerning the California Mission Indians and contribute articles upon the subject to that magazine. She was also commissioned by the Interior Department "to visit the Mission Indians of California, and ascertain the location and condition of the various bands."

She learned of the unrighteous treatment of the Temecula Indians by the white man and of the brutal murder of Juan Diego by Sam Temple. Her very soul was aflame. She was writing magazine articles and recording facts for the joint report rendered by her and Mr. Abbot Kinney to the Department of the Interior. All the pitiful story she was to give to the public. She so asserted repeatedly. It may have been that while in California she did not wish her plan to write a novel to be known, but before her departure she did announce and discuss giving the Mission Indian situation to the public. At one time she intended to tell the story in an appendix to a new edition of her "A Century of Dishonor."

The statements of Señora de Coronel, Mrs. Jackson's most intimate friend in California, and of Mr. Sandham, her artist companion, must be accepted as conclusive proof that Mrs. Jackson did, before departing from California in 1883, conceive and announce the writing of a book which would contain the facts of the inhuman treatment of the Mission Indians by the white man, and to clothe the story with romance.

Mrs. Jackson desired to write the story of the Mission Indians while in Southern California, in the atmosphere of the Coronel home, and within easy reach of reinforcing material; but fate forbade it. The work was scarcely begun when events dictated a different plan, and a temporary suspension of the writing. She realized that unless the Government could be prevailed upon to extend speedy relief to the Indians great suffering would ensue, and she hastened to Washington to lay the whole matter before the President and Congress. She was fortified with reports of officials and civilians, with statements of influential people of all stations, the material facts verified under oath, and was in every way equipped for an effective campaign. She successfully appealed to some of the most prominent men in public

RAMONA LUBO WEEPING AT THE GRAVE OF HER HUSBAND, JUAN DIEGO, CAHUILLA

THE BELLS AND CROSS AT CAMULOS,
NEAR THE CHAPEL

life at the time, including Senator Henry M. Teller of Colorado, and finally prevailed upon the Administration to send out a commission to see what could be done.

Reforms in the policy of the Indian bureau soon followed, and within a twelvemonth she had the satisfaction of securing the passage of a law granting land in severalty, together with implements for its cultivation, to such Indians as would give up their tribal relations. The Indian Rights Association seconded her every effort, also sending a commission to Southern California and doing effective work at Washington.

Before leaving Los Angeles, Mrs. Jackson, in conjunction with the Coronels, devised a somewhat ambitious plan for the institution at some place in Southern California of an industrial school for the Indians, with the idea that many of those who had lost their homes might, with proper instruction, become self-sustaining. It was hoped that the Government would provide a suitable home for such an institution, vesting the title in the Indians, and this achieved, it was her purpose to raise the necessary funds for equipping it by private subscription and otherwise. Personally she contemplated devoting the royalties received from her books to this purpose.

Her mission to Washington accomplished, she went to New York, finished "Ramona," and arranged for its publication. She then began the preparation of five additional books, which she seems to have carried forward simultaneously; but, on account of the fatal illness that attacked her, never completed any of them.

In the midst of this labor of love she was forced to lay down her pen and return to California, her physician hoping but scarcely believing that the change would prolong her life. She survived but a few months, passing away peacefully at San Francisco on the 12th of August, 1885.

The details of her burial on the slopes of Cheyenne Mountain, under the shadow of Pike's Peak, and amidst scenes she loved so much, are familiar topics.

In "California of the South" it is related that in June, 1887, an agent from Washington and several members of the Indian Rights Association from Los Angeles and Pasadena, had a conference with the Indian chiefs, or captains, as they were then called, at Pala Mission, to explain the provisions of the bill,

OLD MISSION INDIANS AND DON ANTONIO

Meeting of Old Mission Indians with Don Antonio de Coronel at Pala, June 28, 1887, with reference to the loss of their lands. Those sitting down had no homes left. "The Indians gathered anxiously around. Each one hat in hand * * * listening attentively to the Hon. A. F. de Coronel, of Los Angeles. * * * When told that he had promised Mrs. Jackson on her death-bed that he would [illegible] visibly affected." *Page 53.*

DON ANTONIO DE CORONEL AND MARIANA, HIS WIFE, ON THE LEFT, LOUISA AND GUITAR PLAYER

which became a law through the efforts of Mrs. Jackson, providing for a division of the reservation lands among the Indians, giving to each one in his individual right one hundred and sixty acres. Pala Mission is twelve miles from Temecula, where the agent and others went on the California Central Railroad.

The meeting is thus described: "At the date of this conference, the apricots and peaches were just ripe, and the orchards were radiant with luscious fruit, that bent many of the boughs almost to the ground. Early on the morning of the conference the Indian chiefs began coming in from the various reservations, the majority on horseback, others in spring-wagons, but all well dressed in the American style. There were captains and generals, quite a number of whom spoke English, Spanish and three or four Indian dialects fluently.

"There were among them several who might have been Alessandros, but no Ramonas. The agent mounted a step of the old Mission, and the Indians gathered anxiously around. Each one had hat in hand, and they all stood there in the hot sun, with bared heads, watching the agent closely as he spoke, and then listening attentively to the Hon. A. F. Coronel, of Los Angeles, as he interpreted the agent's remarks.

There were in this audience some noble faces, to whom the term 'noble red man' could be fittingly applied.

"One noticeable feature was their serious earnestness. They all remembered Mrs. Jackson, who made prolonged visits among them; and when the agent told them that he had promised Mrs. Jackson on her death-bed that he would go on with her work, they were visibly affected.

"Mrs. Jackson's name is familiar to almost every human being in Southern California, from the little three-year-old tot, who has her choice juvenile stories read to him, to the aged grandmother who sheds tears of sympathy for Ramona."

CHAPTER VI

DON ANTONIO FRANCISCO DE CORONEL

ANOTHER generation has come on the stage since Don Antonio de Coronel, the close and helpful friend to Mrs. Jackson, gave up, at the behest of commerce, the picturesque home in the orange grove which had sheltered him and his since 1834. The troubled Mission Indian can no more find it or him. After the partition of the rancho he built a handsome modern residence at the corner of Central Avenue and Seventh Street, Los Angeles, overlooking the old tract, and there, in the companionship of his noble wife, he spent the remainder of his days, dying in 1894.

Helen Hunt Jackson visited the Don and Doña Mariana in 1884, a few months before her death, and there a delegation of Mission Indian women brought to their benefactress, as a token of their love, a beautiful white linen morning robe, marvelously wrought by their own hands, with the drawn work, for which they are famous, accentuating the entire front. Señora de Coronel describes the garment as the most elaborate and exquisite she had ever seen, and calculates that in the production of it months of patient and artistic labor of many persons must have been expended.

To the new home was removed the collection of California antiquities which Don Antonio had been fifty years in gathering, and which has been pronounced unique and the most interesting of any on the coast. California had repeatedly sought to acquire this collection for the exhibit of the State Historical Society, and $30,000 had been offered for it; but this and all other offers were declined, since it had been Doña Mariana's purpose, ever since the death of her husband, to give the precious relics to the city. They were delivered into the care and custody of the Chamber of Commerce of Los Angeles, where they are now displayed, filling entirely one large apartment.

Photographs, sketches and paintings of the old hacienda survive in the Coronel section of the Chamber of Commerce exhibit, and will be viewed with interest and delight by generations yet to come. They give strong hints of the gentle life beneath its expansive eaves in the long ago, when Don Antonio was the Indians' padre and every man's friend, the gates of his castle ever opening inward to all comers, his hospitality known from San Diego to Siskiyou.

The figures depicted in some of these views, those of the old Don and his wholesome, handsome wife, and their native dependents, all drawn from life and perpetuated in oil, will serve to recall not only their charming personalities, but, as well, the gorgeous costuming of that early era on this coast, the chief events of which are rapidly mingling with tradition.

Don Antonio de Coronel was ever the true and faithful friend of the Indians. They trusted him implicitly, and sought him for advice and assistance in all their troubles. Among his last words to his faithful wife was this request: "Mariana, when I am dead and gone, be kind to the Indians. Never turn one away without food."

Chosen as the bearer of captured American flags to the Mexican capital, Don Antonio was chased all over this country by the soldiers of General Kearney, who was determined that the flags should not be sent. Dead or alive, he must be captured, and every inducement was offered the Indians to assist in taking him.

General Kearney promised the Indians that every foot of land taken from them should be restored if only they would deliver up Don Antonio to him. But he had been shrewd enough to dispatch the flags to Mexico by another person, one who would never be suspected of being the bearer. Naturally, however, he did not want to fall into the hands of the Americans. He had other things to do. Upon one occasion a troop of horsemen, under the immediate command of General Kearney, chased him directly to an Indian village; but none of the chiefs knew anything about him, of course. They told him of the offer of General Kearney, but assured him they never would give him up.

Little time was to be lost, and while Kearney was parleying with some of the captains, another rushed Don Antonio out into the cactus patch near by, and beating down the bushes as best he could, pushed Don Antonio beneath them, that he might not be seen, so long as he remained in a crouching position. It was a painful experience he endured, lasting nearly the night through; and when the troopers left, about daylight, he came out a most pitiful sight, his clothing almost stripped from his body, and bleeding at every pore. He was in such a position during all those painful hours that he could not move without encountering the thorns of the cactus. But the Don's life was saved, Indian fidelity was vindicated, and the American flags reached Chapultepec, where they can be seen to-day by the curious.

In "Glimpses of California and the Missions" Mrs. Jackson gives this sketch of Don Antonio de Coronel:

"Don Antonio speaks little English; but the Señora knows just enough of the language to make her use of it delicious, as she translates for her husband. It is an entrancing sight to watch his dark, weather-beaten face, full of lightning changes as he pours out torrents of his nervous, eloquent Spanish speech; watching his wife intently, hearkening to each word she uses, sometimes interrupting her urgently with, 'No, no; that is not it,'—for he well understands the tongue he cannot or will not use for himself. He is sixty-five years of age, but he is young; the best waltzer in Los Angeles to-day; his eye keen, his blood fiery quick; his memory like a burning-glass bringing into sharp light and focus a half-century as if it were a yesterday. Full of sentiment, of an intense and poetic nature, he looks back to the lost empire of his race and people on the California shores with a sorrow far too proud for any antagonisms or complaints. He recognizes the inexorableness of the laws under whose workings his nation is slowly, surely giving place to one more representative of the age. Intellectually he is in sympathy with progress, with reform, with civilization at its utmost; he would not have had them stayed or changed, because his people could not keep up and were not ready. But his heart is none the less saddened and lonely.

"This is probably the position and point of view of most cultivated Mexican men of his age. The suffering involved in it is inevitable. It is part of the great, unreckoned price which must always be paid for the gain the world gets when the young and strong supersede the old and weak.

"A sunny little southeast corner room in Don Antonio's house is full of the relics of the time when he and his father were foremost representatives of ideas and progress in the City of the Angels, and taught the first school that was kept in the place. This was nearly a half-century ago. On the walls of the room still hang maps and charts which they used; and carefully preserved, with the tender reverence of which only poetic natures are capable, are still to be seen there the old atlases, primers, catechisms, grammars, reading-books, which

CHIEF JOSÉ PACHITO AND HIS CAPTAINS AT PALA, JULY, 1885, TO MEET ANTONIO DE CORONEL

DON ANTONIO DE CORONEL SINGING TO HIS WIFE, MARIANA. (*Permission of Miss Annie B. Picher, Pasadena.*)

"Don Antonio would take up his guitar, and, in a voice still sympathetic and full of melody, sing an old Spanish love-song. Never * * * in his most ardent youth could his eyes have gazed on his fair sweetheart's face with a look of greater devotion than that with which they now rest on the noble, expressive countenance of his wife." (Mrs. Jackson in "*Glimpses of California and the Missions.*")

meant toil and trouble to the merry, ignorant people of that time."

Mrs. Jackson then proceeds to relate several stories of the experiences of Don Antonio, after which she continues:

"Sitting in the little corner room, looking out through the open door on the gay garden and breathing its spring air, gay even in mid-winter, and as spicy then as the gardens of other lands are in June, I spent many an afternoon listening to such tales as this. Sunset always came long before its time, it seemed, on these days.

"Occasionally, at the last moment, Don Antonio would take up his guitar, and, in a voice still sympathetic and full of melody, sing an old Spanish love-song, brought to his mind by thus living over the events of his youth. Never, however, in his most ardent youth, could his eyes have gazed on his fairest sweetheart's face with a look of greater devotion than that with which they now rest on the noble, expressive countenance of his wife, as he sings the ancient and tender strains. Of one of them I once won from her, amid laughs and blushes, a few words of translation:—

"'Let us hear the sweet echo
Of your sweet voice that charms me.

The one that truly loves you,
He says he wishes to love;
That the one who with ardent love adores you,
Will sacrifice himself for you.
Do not deprive me,
Owner of me,
Of that sweet echo
Of your sweet voice that charms me.'

"Near the western end of Don Antonio's porch is an orange tree, on which were hanging at this time twenty-five hundred oranges, ripe and golden among the glossy leaves. Under this tree my carriage always waited for me. The Señora never allowed me to depart without bringing to me, in the carriage, farewell gifts of flowers and fruit; clusters of grapes, dried and fresh; great boughs full of oranges, more than I could lift. As I drove away thus, my lap filled with bloom and golden fruit, canopies of golden fruit over my head, I said to myself often: 'Fables are prophecies. The Hesperides have come true.'"

CHAPTER VII

MRS. JACKSON'S HOME AT COLORADO SPRINGS—INDIAN ENVIRONMENTS—THE UTES AND OTHER TRIBES—A FESTIVAL IN HER HONOR

WRITERS without number have time and again sought for the inspiration of "Ramona" in a score or more of historical facts, incidents and circumstances, from the pitiful story of the eviction of the Poncas to the tearful episode at Temecula, stretching across the continent and covering half a century of time. But Helen Hunt Jackson needed none of these. She knew the whole sorrowful story by heart, and from her own windows in her modernized tepee at the corner of Kiowa and Comanche streets, in Colorado Springs, she could have drawn sufficient inspiration for a dozen stories. And it is not a little significant that her own home site should have been on a street corner named for two tribes that regarded Manitou as a shrine, and annually visited it to purify their sin-sick souls and cleanse their bodies.

From the spacious corner apartment, furnished and beautified with articles from her New England home, transplanted to the banks of the Fountaine, every vestige of modern furnishings had been removed. Floor and wall coverings, originally soft rugs from Turkey and Arabia, and tapestries from the banks of the Seine, had given place to bright colored Navajo blankets and flaming Arapahoe and Cheyenne serapes from Arizona and New Mexico. Dainty specimens of the plastic art from the Sèvres works at Paris or the royal plant at Dresden had yielded to the ruder, but perhaps not less spiritual and intellectual creations of the Hopi Indians of Santa Fe. Arab curiosities from the kiosks of Cairo, and French curios from the shops of the Palais Royal had been taken away, that room might be found for Apache bows and arrows and Sioux war-clubs, for samples of those exquisitely wrought baskets of the Mission Indians of California, and unique bits of pottery from the Yaquis of Sonora.

Place had been found, space abundantly conspicuous too, for specimens of drawn work, for which the tribal women of Saboba were and yet are particularly noted. The entire apartment bore an aspect of unmistakable, if unintended, barbaric splendor.

BEAUTIFUL FALLS OF COLORADO

(1) Seven Falls, Colorado, favorite retreat of Helen Hunt Jackson. (2) Ramona Falls, Colorado, named in honor of Helen Hunt Jackson. (3) Rainbow Falls, Colorado, greatly admired and often

DON ANTONIO DE CORONEL IN HIS ORATORY

The crucifix was his mother's and he died with it in his hands. The penitential bracelet, *cilicio*, was on the arm of Father Zalvidea, San Gabriel Mission, when the latter died.

There were in the large collection no baskets made by Ramona; because there never was a Ramona, save in the mind of the gifted author, nor did she ever pretend that there was.

Every article, however, had for its owner a particular language, and each to her told a story peculiarly its own. There was not an item visible that to her lacked deep significance. Few, if any, of the stories they told were bright or cheerful. Most of them were written in blood, and told of the anguish of a race run to earth. Each was treasured for the message it bore of gratitude, simple yet deeply sincere, for acts instinct with love and sympathy.

Long before the ice-mantled crest of Pike's Peak became a landmark for the argonaut in his cross-continent trek to the gold-lined shores of Cherry Creek it served another and broader purpose. To the native Indian tribes of all the vast stretches of mountain and plain radiating from it in all directions it indicated the location of both sanitarium and sanctuary, at the base of those titanic elevations since known to the white man as Pike's Peak, Cameron's Cone and Cheyenne Mountain.

The great Ute Iron Spring and its near neighbor, the Cheyenne Soda Spring, companioned by numerous other bubbling springs without hint of mineral content, had been sought by the afflicted of all the tribes for ages, and had come to be regarded as possessing supernatural curative powers.

These really marvelous springs nestle here and there amidst the rocks and crags and scrub oaks in the sylvan nook at the base of Pike's Peak. They once constituted the red man's sanitarium, belonging to all alike, with no attempt to monopolize their virtues for this tribe or that—the gift of the gods to all who sought relief from physical ills by drinking of or bathing in their wondrous waters.

Scarce a mile away to the eastward was the red man's sanctuary, the Garden of the Gods, where they annually gathered to perform their peculiarly weird religious ceremonies. This interesting bit of nature, in its most freakish mood, embraces four square miles in the charming valley of the Fountaine Que Bouille. Its attractions are most unique, consisting of an immense and varied collection of eroded sandstone rocks, supposedly formed by the winds, into strange figures and grotesque shapes, resembling ruined temples, forts and castles, forms of birds, insects, animals and even of human beings. Conspicuous among these is a particular rock of gigantic proportions and peculiar formation, pointed out to visitors as the one formerly worshiped by the Indians as the Great Manitou—God—giving appropriate name to the locality.

Stretching for miles to the southward along the Front Range is the sweeping slope of Cheyenne Mountain, its face beautified here and there by numerous waterfalls, ever dancing in the golden sunlight from grassy summit to carpeted feet. These mingle in a common outlet, which winds its way through the broad valley and loses itself in the arroyos below. This wondrously beautiful stream of purest mountain water, eternally refreshed from the spotless snow deposits of the upper altitudes, and more or less of a cataract in the rainy season, rejoices in the poetic title of Fountaine Que Bouille.

Beginning at the Garden of the Gods, and extending a distance of forty miles to the westward, is a typical mountain trail, known far and wide as Ute Pass. Winding its tortuous way over the Front Range, its greatest elevation exceeding 12,000 feet, it leads into the South Park, one of the three great natural mountain depressions into which the State of Colorado is divided, sixty miles from north to south, perhaps thirty to forty from east to west, and formerly a great rendezvous for buffalo, elk, deer and antelope—the Indians' hunting ground.

Quite as interesting and remarkable as the natural features already mentioned may be added Monument Park, Glen Eyrie, Cave of the Winds and a hundred others, not less captivating to the eye or rendered less interesting by reason of Indian legend that yet retains hold upon the imagination, although the sway of the pale face has been complete for well nigh half a century.

Necessarily these are here dismissed with a passing word, the main object of their brief mention being achieved in picturing the environment selected by Helen Hunt Jackson for her home, an environment distinctively aboriginal. True, the last Indian had long been driven from his sanitarium and his sanctuary when Mrs. Jackson located at Colorado Springs and took up her life's work there; but natural objects, names, history and legends remained, as ever they will. Every influence suggested the past and its saddening story of broken treaties, of forcible evictions, of wantonly cruel, unchristian, unmerciful treatment of the red man, primary owner of it all.

From this environment Mrs. Jackson looked

out of windows and across bits of landscape, not so long before the sole possession of the Indian, now Indian in name only. Far back had the original possessor been driven, leaving only legendary title upon particular landmarks. In the distance was Cheyenne Mountain, but the Indian tepee was upon its wooded slopes no longer. Winding up over the giant mountain in narrow, tortuous course, was Ute Pass, marking the weary way taken by sad-faced Utes when finally driven from the great spring where they and their forefathers for generations past had gathered to seek surcease from pain in its curative waters. In the foreground was the Garden of the Gods, each sculptured monument full of the deepest significance to Indian mind and heart, surcharged, as the pale face may not begin to realize, with spiritual thoughts and inspirations.

Glen Eyrie would ever remain dear to them as the home of the eagle, perched as it was almost beyond rifle range in the rocky clefts above, and yet undisturbed. There also was the singular " Gateway " to the Garden of the Gods, also full of significance to the aborigines —two lofty spires pointing heavenward; one of the brightest red sandstone, the other of the purest white limestone. There were the Seven

Falls, Bridal Veil Falls, the pearly Fountaine Que Bouille, all differently named by the red man before white occupation, but losing nothing of significance by change in nomenclature. These and a hundred other as unique monuments have been left to mark the "happy hunting grounds" of the long ago.

The Indians themselves had first been forced back of the Front Range into the great South Park, and would have been content to remain there; but the white man quickly followed, uncovered gold along the banks of Chicago Creek and it no longer remained a fit place for the Indian; for the big game went out with the coming in of the whites. Farther back the original possessor must go and seek sustenance at the head waters of the Arkansas. There, too, the white man followed, again discovering fabulous auriferous wealth in the sands of California Gulch; and again the red man must go. Ever backward must he move; away from the great game preserves, away from abundant water supply, away from the gold and silver deposits.

Over the main range was he now forced, where buffalo were not, and where it then was believed nothing more could be found to excite the white man's cupidity; but the red face was scarcely located there when mineral springs larger and more valuable than those at Manitou were found, where coal veins greater than the entire superficial area of Pennsylvania were uncovered, where the great silver ledge at Aspen was located.

It was not long before the Government was importuned again to force the Indian back upon a new frontier, and a wretched place was found for him amidst the wastes of Northwestern Utah. There the Uintah reservation was established, and the trek across another range of mountains directed from Washington. But before the order for removal came the greedy white man had forced himself upon the Indian's new reservation and taken possession.

The chairman of the Senate Committee on Indian Affairs, Mr. Dawes of Massachusetts, from his seat in the Senate, about this time, read to the astonished senators a "proclamation," printed on cloth and tacked on the trees all over the Grand River Reservation, announcing that the Government, by proposing to give the land to the Indians, had parted with its title, and that, inasmuch as "the undersigned," four audacious adventurers, of whom one of the authors of this volume was one, announced that the Indian title would not be recognized, and that anybody wanting anything on the reservation must see them! These four men had located the town-site of Glenwood, the valuable springs adjacent, and about everything else in sight, assigned their "holdings" to an incorporated company, and begun the sale of lots and mines. All this before the Indians had so much as been consulted as to whether they would again consent to move on.

Since the death of Mrs. Jackson and her interment upon the slopes of Cheyenne Mountain, the people of Colorado Springs and Manitou have taken a deep and absorbing interest in commemorating her work, as well as perpetuating the legendary Indian history of what has come to be known as the "Pike's Peak Region." In 1912 an organization was formed for the purpose of giving an annual celebration or carnival, distinctively Indian in all its features. That the fullest recognition of this might be given to the event it is called "Shan Kive" (Indian for fete or carnival, and pronounced "Shawn Keedie").

At the first Shan Kive, in the autumn of 1912, the Ute Pass was formally dedicated. Various Indian dances were indulged in, as well as Indian pony races in costume, and all of the sports and games of the several tribes of

PADRO PABLO, HIS WIFE, AND OTHER MISSION INDIANS, AT HIS HOME AT PAUMA, JULY, 1885

GATEWAY TO THE GARDEN OF THE GODS

MAJOR DOMO. GLEN EYRIE

YUTE PASS AND RAINBOW FALLS, COLORADO

red men who originally owned and inhabited that section, constituted interesting and pleasing features of the occasion. Films were made of all the principal events, and these have been exhibited in all sections of the country.

Primarily intended to exploit the passing race of red men, and to commemorate the great work of "the first lady of Colorado Springs," Helen Hunt Jackson, the event sprang into instant favor. It now occurs annually the first week in September, when Colorado's wonderful flora is at its best, and when the weather in the sun-kissed city is reliably climatic perfection.

The annual celebration of Shan Kive doubtless will serve for many generations, if not for all time, to keep fresh in the minds and hearts of the people the almost sublime work of Helen Hunt Jackson.

CHAPTER VIII

INVESTIGATING THE MISSION INDIANS—THE MEEKER TRAGEDY—"RAMONA" AND "UNCLE TOM'S CABIN"

THE disheartened little woman, Mrs. Jackson, in her modernized tepee at Colorado Springs, had written "A Century of Dishonor," and was at that time wondering why it had failed to stir a Christian nation to action. She was brooding over what seemed to be the failure of its mission. She had repeatedly been to the capital of the nation, and there had met with a reception none too cordial. She was planning the story of "Ramona," little realizing what a great work she was undertaking. Physically she was worn to a frazzle. Mentally she was well-nigh distracted. She had but recently completed a tour of Southern California, using carriage, wagon and burros, enduring all manner of hardships, since in all the vast empire traversed there were no suitable accommodations for a lady of her age, habits of life and refinement.

In this mission she had taken nothing for granted. Wherever there were known to be gathered half a dozen Indians, there she repaired, to look into their condition and to see for herself what might be done for their immediate needs. Thus in turn she was driven to Saboba, Cahuilla, Warner's Ranch, San Ysidro, Los Coyotes, San Ysabel, Mesa Grande, Capitan Grande, Sequan, Conejos, Pala, Rincon, Pauma, San Pasquale, La Jolla, Pechanga, San Gorgonio, Camulos, Temecula, Santa Barbara, San Diego, the Desert Reservation and other places.

It should be remembered that the Indian had not in every instance accorded yielding obedience to the white man's behest to "move on." Occasionally he had demurred to the unreasonable demands made upon him. Upon a few occasions, indeed, he had gone upon the warpath and taken a few scalps. But these occasions were rare, and all told would scarce fill a page of history. On the other hand, the story of the wrongs inflicted upon his people by the whites would crowd many volumes to repletion. Sand Creek and like stories of the butcheries of Indians constitute the bloodiest pages of American border narrative. Unfortunately for Mrs. Jackson, the Northern Utes had, about this time, rebelled against the Government, murdered Agent Meeker and carried his wife, daughter Josephine and a companion, Mrs. Price, into the fastnesses of the mountains, holding them as hostages.

This incident gave the red man's enemies an unusual opportunity to demand the complete wiping out of Chief Ouray's band, although that brave and his immediate followers had always distinguished themselves as the friends of the whites. It counted for little that all three women are said to have become the willing consorts of braves of the Ute tribe; that Josephine Meeker had fairly to be torn away from her dusky lover, Chief Persune; that Mrs. Price reluctantly gave up Chief Jack, and that Mrs. Meeker was not willingly restored to her friends in Colorado. Such reports were currently circulated and generally credited. Mrs. Jackson, alone of all the people of Colorado, was left to defend the acts of the Utes, to the story of the provocation for which none but she willingly would listen.

Numerous writers have undertaken to compare the work of Mrs. Jackson with that of Harriet Beecher Stowe, but with very indifferent success. The works of the two gifted authors possibly may be contrasted, but not well compared. For "Uncle Tom's Cabin," as all well informed persons must be aware, there was a ready-made public sentiment. For nearly a century human slavery had been a living and a burning issue. The Anti-Slavery Society had labored long and effectively in preparing the public for such a novel as finally came from the inspired pen of Mrs. Stowe. There long had been a regularly established and securely founded organization in every Northern State, and in not a few there was an "underground railway" prepared for the fleeing bondmen.

Mrs. Stowe's biographer, her own son, says of the immediate success of "Uncle Tom's Cabin": "Neither she nor her husband had the remotest idea of the unique power and interest of the story that was being written. Nor, indeed, did it dawn upon either of them until after the publication of the first edition in book form. Professor Stowe was a very emotional man, and was accustomed to water his wife's literary efforts liberally with his tears; so the fact that he had wept over the bits of brown paper, upon which the first chapter was written, had for them no unusual portent. As to pecuniary gain, he often expressed the hope that she would make enough by the story to buy a new silk dress!"

Although the public mind and heart were prepared for such a publication, it seems that Mrs. Stowe felt impelled to write to Fred Douglass, calling his attention to the fact that it was appearing as a serial in the "National Era." "Uncle Tom's Cabin" was written at various places, at Brunswick, Maine, and at Boston and Andover; and although announced to run but three months, it was not completed for thirteen months, appearing in book form some weeks thereafter. Ten thousand copies were sold within a few days, and over three hundred thousand within a year, and eight power presses running day and night were barely able to keep pace with the demand for it. It was read everywhere, apparently, and by everybody; and the author soon began to hear echoes of sympathy from all over the land. The indignation, the pity, the distress, that had long weighed upon her soul seemed to pass off from her and into the readers of the book.

So successful had the book been that Mrs. Stowe at once set herself to the task of writing "The Key to Uncle Tom's Cabin," followed by "Dred," all upon the same theme, and all of these several works were translated into nearly every tongue and were widely read the world over. The fame of the author became so great that she felt compelled, after the publication of "The Key" and "Dred," to accept the invitation of friends of the cause of emancipation in England to visit that country as their guest. This she did, extending her visits to France, Germany and Switzerland, everywhere received as a world character to be honored and feted, not alone by the poor and the lowly, but as well by royalty itself.

But a far different sentiment awaited the coming of "Ramona." It was unlooked for and unwanted. It was most indifferently received. Nowhere was there sympathy for "H. H." or "her Indians." Mrs. Jackson's nearest neighbors were yet not proselytes to her mission. There was not a newspaper in Colorado that dared to champion her cause; not a man in public life who cared to assert that reason and justice and logic were on her side.

Friendly as the writer for years had been with Mrs. Jackson, a frequent and as he believes always a welcome visitor to her home, he yet recalls, with the deepest regret and remorse and mortification, the fact that he never employed the instrumentalities at hand to defend the woman and her work, save in a literary way and for a literary reason. The "Leadville Chronicle" and "Leadville Herald-Democrat," which he owned and edited at the time, could have been his powerful weapons in her defense. His conversion came long after her death, the result of a re-reading of her many works upon the Indian question and a deeper and more analytical study of her noble purpose.

Coming late in life though it does, there is now nourished a sincere hope that some amends may be made for earlier mistakes and fatal errors of immature judgment.

Before coming to California Mrs. Jackson was aflame with sympathy for the Mission Indians. January 17, 1880, she thus wrote to one of her intimate friends: "I think I feel as you must have felt in the old Abolition days. I cannot think of anything else from night to morning and from morning to night. . . . I believe the time is drawing near for a great change in our policy toward the Indian. In some respects, it seems to me, he is really worse off than the slaves. They did have, in the majority of cases, good houses,

RAMONA'S BEDROOM, CAMULOS

ARCADE ENTRANCE TO CHAPEL, CAMULOS

and they were not much more arbitrarily controlled than the Indian is by the agent on a reservation. He can order a corporal's guard to fire on an Indian at any time he sees fit. He is 'duly empowered by the Government.'"

On September 4, 1884, Mrs. Jackson thus wrote Señor and Señora de Coronel: "I sometimes wonder that the Lord does not rain fire and brimstone on this land, to punish us for our cruelty to these unfortunate Indians."

Four days before her death Mrs. Jackson wrote the following letter to the President of the United States:

To Grover Cleveland,
President of the United States.

Dear Sir,—

From my death-bed I send you a message of heartfelt thanks for what you have already done for the Indians. I ask you to read my "Century of Dishonor." I am dying happier for the belief that it is your hand that is destined to strike the first steady blow toward lifting this burden of infamy from our country, and righting the wrongs of the Indian race.

With respect and gratitude,
Helen Jackson.

CHAPTER IX

PUBLICATION OF REPORT UPON THE INDIANS—AN INDIAN SCHOOL—MRS. JACKSON'S BURIAL PLACE — PERSONAL INTERVIEW — PREPARING FOR "RAMONA"

THE last visit of the writer to Helen Hunt Jackson's home in Colorado Springs was in the summer of 1883. It was in company with the late Ben Steele, the gifted editor of the "Gazette" of that city, also a warm personal friend of Mrs. Jackson, yet one who, for obvious reasons, withheld from her that public encouragement so freely extended in his personal intercourse. The initial edition of "A Century of Dishonor" had been exhausted, and the details of the publication of another were quite generally discussed at this informal gathering.

In July, 1882, Mrs. Jackson had been commissioned by the Secretary of the Interior, together with Mr. Abbot Kinney, of Los Angeles, to visit and report upon the condition of the Mission Indians of California. This recognition by the Government had been highly gratifying to her and she appeared to be deeply appreciative of the assistance rendered her by Mr. Kinney. In subsequent correspondence with him he had invariably addressed her as "General," a circumstance which appealed strongly to her sense of humor. She once wrote that one of her first, if not her very first, resolutions in life was not to be "a woman with a hobby," and here she was being recognized everywhere as a woman with a very pronounced hobby, the Indians, and addressed as "General" by a male companion in official life.

The judgment of those present at this meeting was consulted as to whether it were better to print her report upon the Southern California Indians under separate cover, or as an appendix to another edition of "A Century of Dishonor," at that time deemed imperative. Because of the relative brevity of the joint report upon the condition and needs of the Mission Indians, it was the consensus of opinion of those present that it would be more likely to secure a larger reading by going out as a part of a work that already had passed to a second edition, and that course was agreed upon. But at the same time she announced that she intended writing a novel in which she would present the wretched story of the Mission Indians of California.

It may be here remarked that Mrs. Jackson was not so much displeased with the sale of the original edition of "A Century of Dishonor"; her disappointment related more to the apparent apathy with which it had been received by Senators, members of Congress and bureau officers having charge of Indian affairs. She had under consideration at the time a number of projects calling for governmental recognition and financial support, and doubtless was unduly impatient with the slow processes then in vogue. Her most ambitious scheme was the establishment, at some point in Southern California, of an industrial school for Mission Indian women. For this she desired the Government to donate a suitable site and deed it to the Indians. For its endowment she intended to devote all royalties received from the sale of her several books, including the one just begun, which developed into the great American novel, "Ramona." She looked to the Coronels to aid her in this great undertaking. They were to take charge of this institution.

Mrs. Jackson was at this time an exceedingly busy woman. She was ever that, however, but her official and literary work was crowding her, and she complained that not as often as she desired, and as formerly had been her habit, had she been able to visit her favorite places in the mountains. Chief of these was Cheyenne Mountain and the numerous and beautiful waterfalls for which the locality always has been noted. One of these, and one of the most picturesque, has since been christened "Ramona Falls," for the lovely heroine of the romance. Her favorite, however, was Seven Falls, one of the most beautiful and picturesque in America, the source of which, at that time, was reached by a series of rather steep wooden steps, just upon the edge of the foaming cascade. It was here, at the summit of the mountain crag, in a little grove of spruce trees and near the edge of a huge pile of volcanic rock, that Mrs. Jackson selected a burial place for herself. Her desires in this respect were strictly executed, and for a number of years she rested there, in the place she loved so much, under the shadows of Pike's Peak and within sound of the splashing waters of Seven Falls.

Later, and for a reason not anticipated at the time of her interment, it became necessary to disinter the remains and rebury them at

Evergreen Cemetery, Colorado Springs. A ranchman in Cheyenne Cañon had taken advantage of his title to the land upon which the grave was located to charge an admission fee to see it, and also reaped a considerable revenue from hiring to tourists a burro, once owned and used by Mrs. Jackson upon which to skirt the mountain side.

This commercializing of the grave became so distasteful to the author's relatives and friends, in the course of time, as to make it imperative to remove the remains. They were taken away as quietly and unceremoniously as they had been laid there at her request, and even the local papers were not advised of the incident for some time thereafter.

During the last visit of the writer to the home of Mrs. Jackson she related many interesting incidents of her official journey through the mountains of Southern California, its pleasing as well as its sorrowful phases. She spoke feelingly of the Coronels, and related in what manner they had been most helpful to her. It was at their suggestion and urgent insistence that Mrs. Jackson had paid a visit to Camulos ranch, and all that she said regarding that visit led her hearers to believe that the scene of the novel she had in hand was to be laid there.

Notwithstanding her excessive modesty in referring to the work she had undertaken, it was not difficult to realize that it was her purpose to make it what since it has turned out to be, "the great American novel." Very naturally she preferred to talk about the work already done rather than to speculate upon future plans. The conversation was mainly in regard to "A Century of Dishonor," and the deep disappointment she felt that it had not produced that effect upon the national conscience which she had a right to expect.

It is doubtful if an author ever before had taken such pains as had Mrs. Jackson to prepare for the production of "Ramona." She well knew, long in advance of its publication, that she was not to have a friendly reception for her work. She felt that public criticism would be merciless, and fully realized the importance of unquestioned correctness in every position taken. Her first step had been to thoroughly inform herself regarding the law, the ground work of human rights. She had read everything relating to the lives and characters, the public and private utterances, of such men as Garrison, Whittier, Lowell,

Phillips, Starr King, Lovejoy, Brown and all the other national leaders of the anti-slavery movement. She had read all the treaties with all the American Indian tribes of record, from that with the Delawares in 1620 down to the day and hour when it became necessary to close her narrative, analyzing the conditions and traversing the history of each, never failing to disclose the almost uniform bad faith of the Government in carrying out solemn obligations entered into between a powerful people upon the one side and weak, dependent wards upon the other. She dug up and waded through hundreds of musty public documents, read thousands of pages of the "Congressional Record," and finally entered upon her great task with a full equipment of information pertinent to the subject, a large part of which she found to her mortification was wholly unknown to the executive officers of the Government at the time.

CAMULOS RANCH AND THE HILLS TO THE NORTH

OLIVE MILL, PRESS AND KETTLE, CAMULOS

"Here * * * might still be studied the pressing of the olive in the old morteros." *Page 193.*

CHAPTER X

THE CORONELS—THE "REAL" RAMONA AND HER BASKETS—THE INSPIRATION OF "RAMONA"—CAMULOS RANCH AND ITS CUSTOMS —THE RAMONA JEWELS

MORE than a decade after this last conversation with Helen Hunt Jackson it was the privilege of the writer to visit Southern California. His thoughts naturally were largely of his dead friend and her great work in behalf of the Mission Indians. He assumed that he would be accorded a cordial welcome at the home of Doña Mariana de Coronel, then a widow, and was not disappointed. She was not alone cordial, but communicative to a degree, and in that initial and in subsequent interviews a fund of most interesting and valuable information was disclosed. She regretted that so many fictions had arisen concerning "Ramona," and expressed a desire that someone should undertake to tell the true story.

Some years ago one of the authors of this book prepared a short story upon "Ramona," in which the inspiration and creation of the romance were told, which was published in the "Out West" magazine. In this article the writer endeavored to give some of the real facts surrounding the story, and asserted that the characters of Alessandro and Ramona were fictitious. This declaration was not calculated to encourage the imposition on tourists by curio sellers in palming off baskets as having been made by the Ramona of Helen Hunt Jackson.

The publication of this article was followed by the receipt of an extraordinarily large number of letters from persons in various sections of the country, as well as in Europe, whose ideals had thus been hopelessly demolished. All protested that they had bought their Ramona-made baskets in good faith, treasured them sacredly, and each pronounced it a burning shame that he or she should have been imposed upon by conscienceless traffickers, or that the writer should, at such a late day, attempt to discourage the popular belief in the existence of a real Ramona, and deny that she was still in the business of basket making on a large scale in some impossible cañon down by the sea.

The only comfort that could be extended

these unhappy correspondents was cheerfully given. It was not much, but it at least possessed the quality of sincerity. It was declared by the writer that to his mind nothing could compensate for the exchange of the idealized Ramona, one of the most charming characters fiction has ever donated to the world of letters, for a squat Indian, with straight, coarse black hair, thick lips and high cheek bones, capable of sitting all day in a bamboo wickiup and contenting herself with the weaving of baskets, however beautiful in themselves or symbolic in their conception. At all events, he suggested that a little reflection would have saved these unfortunate investors much of their sentiment and some of their money.

Inasmuch as the time of the story, by comparison of records and incidents, must have been between 1840 and 1880, the life of the "real" Ramona could hardly have been extended, even by the liberal use of Aunt Ri's herb decoctions, down to the twentieth century. And again, if the "real" Ramona were indeed an Indian, and had given her undivided time and talents to the creation of baskets, it would not have been possible, within the space of one short life, to produce the large number that have been purchased for the decoration of the homes of Ramona-lovers all over the country, and that yet comprise so large a proportion of the stock of curio stores all over Ramonaland, from Monterey to San Diego.

The writer came to California with the principal facts regarding the inspiration, progress and completion of the romance thoroughly grounded in his mind. Mrs. Jackson had in substance told him that the Coronels had inspired the story, had aided immensely in the task of gathering material for it, and finally had insisted that she should visit Camulos ranch to secure the necessary local color. Neither Guajome, which she had several times visited, nor any other Southern California ranch was referred to by her in connection with the plot then in her mind for the romance of "Ramona."

Doña Mariana de Coronel confirmed the conviction already entertained regarding the chief incidents, and urged a personal visit to Camulos as almost essential to a correct understanding of all the incidents of the plot.

This latter suggestion was acted upon without unnecessary loss of time. So often had the hospitality of the del Valle household been imposed upon by curiosity-seekers and

CAMULOS RANCH AND THE HILLS TO THE SOUTH

BALCONY AT CAMULOS,

From which Señora del Valle was accustomed to watch for the coming of her husband down the valley It presents a view of many miles.

relic-hunters that a favorable introduction was a thing to be prized. This the writer procured through the long acquaintance and close intimacy of his wife with the family of Senator del Valle of Los Angeles, and a most delightful day was spent within the classic precincts of the real home of the only Ramona that ever existed, the character idealized from the persons of Blanca Yndart and Guadalupe, the little Indian ward of Doña Ysabel del Valle, as heretofore stated.

The writer's wife, some time previously, had spent an entire week as a guest at the ranch, during which she had opportunity to thoroughly familiarize herself with animate and inanimate features of the place. Members of the del Valle family had pointed out the original boundaries of the ranch, exactly corresponding with Mrs. Jackson's description. It had indeed extended "forty miles westward to the sea, forty miles eastward into the San Fernando Mountains, and an equal distance along the coast line."

But Governor Pio Pico's grants had been largely disallowed by the American authorities, when they took over the country, and the limitations of the princely ranch had been greatly circumscribed. The crosses were yet upon the hillsides to the north and the south of the ranch house, that the heretics might still know, "when they go by, that they are on the estate of a good Catholic."

The "aroma of it all lingered there still." It had not been an unusual thing, during Señor del Valle's day, for as many as fifty people to be seated in the spacious dining-room at one time. The working force of the ranch was perhaps never quite so large, but the occasion was rare when a dozen or more guests were not being entertained.

It was a custom at Camulos, as at many another Spanish home in the Mission days, to place a basket of silver money in the room of the passing guest, stranger though he be, that he might replenish the financial needs of his journey.

The resources of the ranch were large and varied, and settlements for wool and fruit and other foodstuffs came in large amounts. These were almost invariably made in coin, and it was the custom of the Señor del Valle to keep all of the funds in a large trunk or box, that was never locked against any member of the family, nor was any account ever kept of the withdrawals made from time to time.

When the writer was there the pay-roll

probably did not include more than a quarter of a hundred. But even from this diminished number in the household it would not have been difficult for the observer to select almost every character of the romance from those gathered in the patio and on the south veranda of the typical old Spanish hacienda. Neither Blanca Yndart, Guadalupe nor Senator del Valle was there. But there was Señora del Valle, still the uncrowned queen of the realm; half-breeds of almost noble bearing, who easily might represent Alessandro; and other personages who, without violent wrenching of the imagination, might be taken for Juan Canito, the chief herder, for Marda, the cook, Anita and Maria, the forty-year-old twins, "born on the place," and their two daughters, Rosa and Anita the Little, for José, and all the other characters of the story. There was present more than one representative of old Juanita, oldest of the household, "silly, and good only to shell beans"; for to the day of her death Señora del Valle maintained a goodly little army of pensioned retainers, none of whom could she think of turning away.

It has long been the custom to hold an annual fiesta at Camulos ranch, a gathering of the del Valle family and friends. A guest at one of these annual gatherings wrote a description of it, published in "California of the South," which is here submitted:

"The annual fiesta is a gathering of the del Valle family and a few invited guests that takes place in July, and lasts four days. The train from Los Angeles arrived about noon of the first day with twenty-five of the family and friends. Señora del Valle stood at the entrance to the garden and welcomed each guest. The visitors were quickly conducted to their rooms, where water, comb and brush soon removed all trace of the midsummer car-ride. Dinner was then announced, and Senator Reginald F. del Valle, a prominent Los Angeles attorney, sat at the head of the table, which was under a shady arbor in the garden but a few steps from the chapel. Two barbecued pigs, done to perfection, formed the principal meat of this meal, but there were olives, cooked and pickled, various Spanish dishes, containing almost invariably chiles (red peppers) and olives, delicious dessert, claret and white wine *ad libitum*, and the regulation black coffee. Surrounding the table were members of numerous distinguished Spanish-American families. The two features that attracted the particular attention of an American were the

THE GRAVEYARD AT CAMULOS

"They bore the Señora to the little graveyard on the hillside, * * * silent and still at last, the [illegible] proud, sad heart." "*Ramona.*"

WHERE THE BROOK AT CAMULOS NOW RUNS

gallantry of the men and the beauty and vivacity of the ladies.

"The afternoon was spent by the guests hunting, riding, singing, reading, talking and mountain-climbing, just as each one chose. In this way of entertaining, and yet giving each visitor perfect freedom to do just as he pleased, the hostess and her daughters displayed rare tact. Watermelons and fruits of various kinds were always at hand.

"At 7 P.M. another bountiful meal was served in the arbor, which was brilliantly lighted by lanterns fastened between the innumerable clusters of purple grapes that hung overhead. This time two roasted kids were served—and delicious they were. After an hour's walk, all gathered in the spacious parlor, and, with music on the piano, the organ and the guitar, and vocal solos and choruses, time quickly sped. Fireworks in the garden closed the entertainment for the first day.

"The next morning all were out bright and happy, and at breakfast, where everything was served with the usual profusion, the American would notice that olives were again eaten by all, which leads to a reflection in regard to the value of this ancient food.

"After breakfast an hour was spent by the

good hostess and her Catholic guests in the chapel.

"A fat young steer was then lassoed by a vaquero, the aorta was dexterously severed with a knife, and then began some dissecting that would have surprised the most skillful anatomist. The skin was quickly and neatly taken off and spread out to protect the beef from the earth; the muscles were then, layer after layer, deftly removed, and in an incredibly short time this Mexican butcher had the meat ready for the fire.

"A fire in a pit near by had been heating stones, which were now red-hot. Iron rods were laid across the pit, and the whole beef put on to roast for dinner.

"The noon train from Los Angeles added materially to the number of guests, and seventy-five as happy people as ever lived sat around the heavily-laden table under the grape-vines. What a delicious meal that was! The eating was happily interspersed with laughter, conversation and brilliant repartee.

"After the dessert had been enjoyed toasts were in order, and following those to the del Valle family, and Southern California, a gray-headed Mexican gentleman, after delivering a fervid, eloquent eulogy upon, proposed a toast to the memory of Helen Hunt Jackson, which was drank standing. How true the statement: 'Mrs. Jackson is dead, but her work still lives in the hearts of the people of Southern California.'"

The Ramona jewels were not exhibited, nor yet referred to, upon this visit of the writer. There was no occasion for it. They had all been given to Blanca Yndart, upon the occasion of her marriage to James Maguire, about 1878. Blanca had removed them, with other belongings, to her home at Newhall, a town midway between Los Angeles and Camulos.

The nomenclature, "Ramona jewels," is misleading, since the property, in addition to jewels, included a large trunk filled to repletion with dress skirts, waists, shawls, bolts of silk and of satin, and female lingerie generally. Most if not all of these were rich and costly, some of them very old, and all highly prized.

It is an habitual practice of the old Spanish families to retain clothing for years, and in the attic of the ranch house at Camulos there were not less than thirty trunks filled with clothing that had been accumulating for generations. Often skirts were made over for the children, but the waists, on account of changing fashions and perhaps for other reasons, could not be so utilized, and in these trunks were samples of the fashions of numerous decades.

The jewel case in the "secret closet" back of the statue of Saint Catherine, to which Señora Moreno is made to point in her dying conversation with Felipe, is the purest myth. There never was such a secret closet in the wall at Camulos, and Mrs. Jackson used it simply to heighten the reader's interest and add to the tensity of the situation.

The Ramona jewels, until removed by Blanca Yndart, remained in a large trunk under the bed in Señora del Valle's chamber. They remained there many years, and there may have been many reasons for so keeping them segregated from the other trunks and boxes. None was volunteered and no explanation invited. Sight of the trunk itself was of more than ordinary interest to the writer. The jewels, as well as some of the rich fabrics, had been seen before. Mrs. Maguire had caused some of the former to be put in more modern settings, and much of the silks and satins had been worked up into garments for herself and children.

The significant fact about the Ramona jewels

is that they correspond almost exactly with the description given of them in "Ramona."

Title to Camulos ranch now vests in the "del Valle Estate," incorporated, and doubtless always will remain an asset of the younger members. At this writing its affairs are being managed by a son, Ulpiano del Valle, the mother having died March 28, 1905.

CHAPTER XI

HON. REGINALD F. DEL VALLE—THE CHARACTER OF FELIPE—THE MISSION PLAY—LUCRETIA LOUISE DEL VALLE—THE "RAMONA" STORY AND THE DEL VALLE FAMILY—OFFENSIVE TOURISTS

TO define a gentleman one might go far afield without disclosing a more pronounced exemplar than is Hon. Reginald F. del Valle, eldest son of Don Ygnacio and Señora del Valle, who of all the human documents yet living is most readily identified as the person Mrs. Jackson had in mind in the idealization of the character of Felipe in the romance. Attire him in Spanish garb, as the artist Henry Sandham has properly done, and the portraits are not wholly unlike.

Senator del Valle left Camulos ranch early in life to prepare himself for the practice of law, a profession he has graced for a quarter of a century in Los Angeles. Without undue self-seeking upon his part he has during that period been honored with many positions of distinction and trust. He always has been a consistent and active member of the Democratic party, ever prominent in its councils, and not infrequently called upon to preside over its state conventions. Once he was a candidate for Lieutenant-Governor of California, at another time he served a term with great credit in the State Senate, securing for Los Angeles the State Normal school, and again was a delegate to the national convention of his party. At this time he is serving the City of Los Angeles in the honorary position of a member of the Municipal Water Board, a most important post during the period of bringing the Owens River to the city's gate. It was understood that, in the event of the election of Mr. Bryan, in 1896, Senator del Valle was to have the post of Ambassador to Mexico.

It is an interesting circumstance, in this connection, that the romance of Mrs. Jackson closes with the arrival and settlement of Felipe and his beautiful bride in the Mexican capital. Of this the author says: "The story of the romance of their lives, being widely rumored, greatly enhanced the interest with which they were welcomed. The beautiful young Señora Moreno was the theme of the city; and Felipe's bosom thrilled with pride to see the gentle dignity of demeanor by which she was distinguished in all assemblages."

In the spring of 1913 affairs throughout the Republic of Mexico were in such chaotic condition, owing to the movements of various revolutionary bodies, that the Administration at Washington felt impelled to withhold recognition of the provisional government represented by General Huerta until reliable assurances could be given of its ability to maintain a stable government and to give adequate protection to the lives and property of all classes of people. That dependable information might be obtained from the various opposing factions in the republic, President Wilson determined to send a personal representative into Mexico, to report such facts as might be developed directly to him, to the end that such action as might finally be taken by the government of the United States should be based upon indisputable facts, gathered by a person wholly disinterested. The mission was a peculiarly delicate one, calling for the highest order of intelligence, of tact and diplomacy. That the distinction should fall upon Hon. Reginald Francisco del Valle, of California, was not calculated to surprise anyone, since his entire fitness for the trust was and is universally recognized.

Senator del Valle, his wife and daughter

A WINDOW IN RAMONA'S BEDROOM, CAMULOS DWELLING

All are barred. "It had been a long, sad day for Ramona, and as she sat in her window * * * and looked at Alessandro pacing up and down, she felt for the first time * * * that she was glad he loved her" "*Ramona.*"

HON REGINALD F DEL VALLE,

The eldest son of the mistress of Camulos ranch, the same relation as Felipe to Señora Moreno of "Ramona."

accompanying him, went to Mexico, and at this writing he is in the City of Mexico, performing the duty assigned him by the President of the United States.

This mission to the capital of Mexico calls vividly to mind the consummation of the story of "Ramona." Felipe and Ramona, with the latter's infant daughter, went to Monterey, where they boarded a vessel and sailed for Mexico City, and were there married and lived.

The somewhat phenomenal presentation of "The Mission Play," Mr. John S. McGroarty's magnificent and educational creation, at old San Gabriel, near Los Angeles, daily during the spring and summer of 1913, and later in San Francisco and other cities, has significance in this connection from the circumstance that the title role was assumed by Miss Lucretia Louise del Valle, the only child of the Senator, and the further fact that the old garret at Camulos contributed very largely to the young lady's strikingly beautiful native wardrobe, deemed essential to the proper presentation of the play.

In enacting the leading feminine role Miss del Valle is appareled to represent the Spanish dress style of 1847. The costly and elaborate dress she wears in the character belonged to her grandmother, Señora del Valle, and the beautiful shawl that adorns her shoulders was given to the grandmother by her grandfather in 1852, when the latter was a member of the California legislature. The coiffure worn by her also belonged to the grandmother, and was the style of dressing the hair in 1847.

Senator del Valle has related to the authors the effect of "Ramona" on his mother's family. They suffered in two ways, he said. The public accepted his mother, Señora del Valle, the widowed owner of Camulos ranch, as the original of the character of Señora Moreno of the romance, and to her were attributed all the faults, imperfections and eccentricities of Señora Moreno. Public prejudice and criticism were harshly directed toward the noble and saintly Señora del Valle, who was in life the direct opposite of Señora Moreno in the latter's hatred and cruelty of Ramona. The authors especially refer the reader to the chapter in this volume of which Señora del Valle is the subject.

For several years subsequent to the publication of "Ramona," 1884, tourist excursions to California were mainly those conducted by a Boston firm, and were composed of New England people. Camulos ranch, the home of Ra-

SEÑORA DOÑA YSABEL DEL VALLE.

The widowed mistress of Camulos ranch, accepted as Señora Moreno of "Ramona."

MISS LUCRETIA LOUISE DEL VALLE,

Daughter of Senator R. F del Valle, and granddaughter of the mistress of Camulos ranch, appareled as she appears in the leading feminine rôle of Mr John S. McGroarty's magnificent production, the Mission Play, San Gabriel, California, 1913. The fan, coiffure, shawl and dress were owned by Señora del Valle, the grandmother, and show the Spanish style of dress of 1847

mona, was one of the California places of greatest interest to them; and, by special arrangement, the Southern Pacific train stopped at the ranch for a sufficient time to permit the tourists to visit the home of Ramona.

Senator del Valle yet grows indignant when talking of the conduct of the New Englanders. They were rude, he asserts, and wholly ill-mannered. They picked the flowers and fruit, swarmed over the yard and gardens, took valuable articles for souvenirs, and invaded the dwelling uninvited; and, on one occasion, when in the room described in the novel as having been the sleeping apartment of Ramona, a woman threw herself on the bed, exclaiming, "Now I can say I have laid on Ramona's bed."

Such unseemly and rough conduct resulted in the ranch being closed to the Boston firm's excursionists, Senator del Valle himself writing the order to the firm, and declaiming against the perpetration of "Boston manners," as he put it, on Camulos ranch.

At this time parties are courteously and graciously permitted to enter the ranch at the old dwelling; but they are expected to demean themselves properly.

CHAPTER XII

DOÑA YSABEL DEL VALLE—THE MISTRESS OF CAMULOS RANCH—SEÑORA MORENO OF "RAMONA"

CAMULOS ranch has by universal acclaim been accepted as the home of Ramona. The evidence conclusively establishes this fact. Naturally we turn there for the originals of the principal characters of the novel.

We have heretofore asserted that Blanca Yndart and Guadalupe, the Indian girl, both wards of Señora del Valle, the mistress of Camulos, most likely suggested to Mrs. Jackson, in the blending of their lives, the character of Ramona, and that Reginald F. del Valle, the eldest son of the family, could truly be taken as the original of Felipe.

What Mrs. Jackson did not see or hear of the del Valle household when at Camulos was detailed to her by the Coronels. The fact that she did not meet Señora del Valle, because of the latter's absence from home on a mission of mercy elsewhere, weighed but little. Mrs.

Jackson let nothing escape her. She tenaciously and retentively sought full knowledge of every person and thing that were incident to her travels.

On meeting the Coronels after her visit to Camulos ranch, Mrs. Jackson was gleeful and enthusiastic over her trip there. She wanted all possible information concerning Señora del Valle, her deceased husband, Blanca Yndart, Guadalupe, Reginald F. del Valle, the eldest son, and other members of the household, and of the customs of the ranch.

The strong religious part of the personality of Señora del Valle was pictured to Mrs. Jackson by the Coronels, who knew that devout woman intimately; and it may be correctly asserted that the religious devotion portrayed in the character of Señora Moreno was suggested by the saintly and religious life of Señora del Valle.

But the harsh and unlovable disposition of Señora Moreno—her haughty, merciless and cruel nature which crushed Ramona and drove her out into the night with an Indian sheep-shearer—was never intended by Mrs. Jackson to be attributed to Señora del Valle, whose disposition, charity, nobleness and sympathy were the beautiful gems in her sweet character.

Mrs. Jackson desired it to be distinctly understood that she was not writing history in giving to the world the story of "Ramona." Nowhere in the novel does she specify Camulos ranch by name. The character of Señora Moreno was of her own creation, into whose life were injected these features of Señora del Valle: widowhood, the owner and mistress of an old California hacienda, devoutness to the Catholic Church, and having a son within the description of the magnanimous character of Felipe.

And it is because Mrs. Jackson drew from Señora del Valle the good qualities given to Señora Moreno of "Ramona," that makes the former an important and interesting personage in the story of "Ramona." And it was Señora del Valle who was the mistress of Camulos ranch, who maintained the chapel there, from whose dress the torn altar cloth was made, who maintained the Mission bells, whose hospitality was extended to all who came upon her estate, and who "caused to be set up upon every one of the soft rounded hills which made the beautiful rolling sides of that part of the valley, a large wooden cross, . . . that the faithful may be reminded to pray."

Señora Ysabel del Valle was one of the noblest women ever created, distinguished far and wide for those characteristics that made her life a distinct blessing to all with whom she came in contact, and her death a loss from which a wide community has not yet ceased to suffer acutely or to mourn without surcease.

In older times saints were made of such material; and were we living in the fourteenth rather than the twentieth century we certainly would have a Saint Ysabel.

So true, so sincere, so devout, so constant, was her devotion to the Church of Rome, that when she died Bishop Conaty of Los Angeles took it upon himself to make all the arrangements for the funeral, saying to the family, "she belongs to *us*, not to *you*, and the Church claims all the privileges of caring for its own."

From "The Tidings," the authorized organ of the Catholic Church of the Los Angeles diocese, we take the following concerning Señora del Valle and her funeral:

"Señora del Valle was the daughter of Don Cerval Varela and Doña Ascencion Avila. Don Varela took an active part in the war with the United States and led an attack against the Americans at Rancho del Chino. He was the possessor of large tracts of land on which is now Boyle Heights and was owner of the site where the Catholic orphanage now stands.

"Señorita del Varela married Don Ygnacio del Valle, a man prominent in the history of California, and who controlled many of the large ranches in the San Fernando Valley. The ceremony was performed at the Church of Our Lady of the Angels, Los Angeles, December 14, 1851.

"As the funeral cortege passed the orphan asylum on Boyle Heights three hundred or more of the children of that institution, dressed in white, stood in line by the roadside and recited aloud the prayers for the dead.

"To the few mourners who had lived in the early days and whose minds were treasured with the memories of Señora del Valle's youth, who had witnessed the trend of her young life as it molded itself into the woman and she became known as an exemplar among a people where the reign of honor and hospitality seemed to reach no bounds, the spectacle of these motherless children appealed most strikingly, and the days of the old Camulos were again recalled; days when great herds of stock wandered over the hills and valleys of the famous rancho, and the orchards hung heavy with the products of the fruitful seasons.

POMEGRANATE TREES, CAMULOS, 1913

ARCADE ENTRANCE TO CAMULOS CHAPEL

"This chapel was dearer to the Señora than her house." "*Ramona.*"

"Life was much the same at Camulos as on the other great ranchos, and as the travel-worn stranger passed on his journey, by horse or afoot, he stopped for a while at the household where a welcome was never wanting.

"The mistress of the rancho attended personally to the details of the home-life, and from the break of dawn when the chapel bells called all to the morning devotion, she watched over her family and the servants of the household with a firmness and gentleness of manner which won a love and respect that time has never altered.

"Instances of Señora del Valle's charity are innumerable, and race or creed did not enter into her thoughts when, whatever the hour of need, she was called upon to care for the poor or distressed.

"She had been removed to Los Angeles several years before her death, where she made her home with her daughter, Mrs. Josefa Forster, at whose residence she died. In her last moments she begged to be taken to Camulos that she might die amid scenes which were the dearest to her on earth, where her children had been raised and where her husband was lying under the altar of the little chapel."

"The Tidings" is mistaken as to the burial

place of the husband of Señora del Valle. He was buried in the family graveyard at Camulos, but his remains were afterward removed and reinterred in the Catholic Cemetery at Los Angeles.

At the close of the funeral exercises after the absolution, Rt. Rev. Bishop Conaty said:

"While it is contrary to the established rules of the parish to deliver a eulogy over the dead, I feel that this occasion is one which will allow the rule to be set aside out of respect for the memory of the services rendered religion by the good woman whose death is universally lamented.

"She represented a type of womanhood, the glory of the Church, as well as of the community in which it is found. She was a woman whose life was dominated by the spirit of absolute and simple faith, which led her through a long life to untold deeds of kindness and charity. Her faith was something more than profession; it expressed itself in the everyday act of religion and charity.

"Her home was the center of her affections, and the love of husband and children caught its glow from the love of God, which characterized her entire life. The ranch home at Camulos was the home of hospitality and the

THE ROSARY OF THE DEL VALLE FAMILY.

Made of the first gold found in California. (*Permission of Miss Annie B. Picher, Pasadena.*)

center of the religious life of all who came in contact with it. Her love of faith led her to a love for the altar and the priesthood, and the first gift of her olive harvest was in the oil needed for the Holy Thursday consecration in the Diocesan Cathedral.

"As a young woman, wife and mother, the Señora of Camulos was a model of Christian womanhood, and she leaves the sweetest memories of all that stands for goodness of life in Christian virtue. This type of woman is the outcome of faith in the Church which she loved. It is needed in our civilization to teach us the beauty of home-life in which the service of God is the source and spirit of God, the inspiration. Such women are the bulwarks of our civilization and the pride of our humanity."

To the smallest detail Señora del Valle was buried as a church dignitary would have been, and when asked for the expense bill by a family well able and more than willing to pay, the members of it were denied the privilege of participating even in that.

After Don Ygnacio del Valle passed away, and until her own death, Señora del Valle was never seen with uncovered head. The nature of her husband's illness had been such that he could not lie down with comfort, and he died while sitting in a chair. His devoted wife sat close to and directly in front of him, and when the final moment came and the last flickering spark of life went out, his head gently dropped upon that of his wife, their foreheads meeting. The Señora wore at the time a light mantilla, a custom of Spanish ladies. Her husband's life had gone out while his head rested upon it, and thereafter this covering was never removed, day or night, save upon a few occasions when it became necessary to replace it temporarily with a bonnet. This circumstance accentuates the Señora's unyielding devotion to whatever she regarded as a sacred duty.

CHAPTER XIII

THE ORIGINALS OF THE CHARACTERS OF "RAMONA"

IT may be correctly asserted that nearly every character of "Ramona" had its original, either in whole or in part. Mr. Abbot Kinney was a co-commissioner with Mrs. Jackson in an official investigation into the condition of the Mission Indians of Southern California. Referring to their joint report to the Secretary of the Interior, Mr. Kinney says: "It was made by Mrs. Jackson and myself, and it was in the investigations that led to the making of it that the book 'Ramona' was born. We actually saw some of the incidents described; many of the facts were developed by the witnesses, all of whom we examined under oath. We met with many of the characters whose pictures were afterwards drawn with startling fidelity by Mrs. Jackson in the pages of her book."

Mr. Henry Sandham, the "Century's" artist, who accompanied Mrs. Jackson on her journeys through Southern California, wrote thus: "As for the characters themselves, I have now in my possession sketches and studies made from life at the time of meeting the originals, meetings that were often as much fraught with meaning for me as they were for Mrs. Jackson."

In other chapters of this volume it is stated that the character of Señora Moreno was suggested to Mrs. Jackson in part by Doña Ysabel del Valle, widowed mistress of Camulos ranch; that Ramona was a blending of two members of the del Valle family, Blanca Yndart, a Spanish girl, now Mrs. James Maguire, residing with her daughter at Los Angeles, and Guadalupe, a Mission Indian girl, given to Señora del Valle when a child by a Piru chief; and that in Felipe was the portrayal of the eldest son of the mistress of Camulos ranch, Don Reginald Francisco del Valle. Guadalupe is married and now resides in Arizona.

Alessandro

It has been a vain search to identify any living person as Alessandro. Sheep-shearing bands in Southern California were numerous at the time laid for the story, and each had its captain.

In the Coronel Collection at the Los Angeles Chamber of Commerce is a photograph of Rojerio Rocha, choir leader at San Fernando Mission and a violin player, whose lands were shamefully appropriated by white men, one of whom is now a well-to-do and prominent resident of Los Angeles. This Indian singer and violinist was well known to the Coronels, and they told Mrs. Jackson of him in detail. He has been declared by many to have suggested the character of Alessandro.

Like Alessandro, Rojerio was a violin player and a singer. He played from notes and had a fine voice, the finest in the old Mission choir. The old people about the Mission even now tell of the wonderful playing of the violin by Rojerio.

He was also an expert blacksmith and silversmith, and performed both services at the Mission for many years. He formed much of the beaten gold and silver plate used by the Mission fathers, and it was his skill that fashioned the elaborately silver-ornamented bridles used by the wealthy señores of the Mission days.

Rojerio married and continued to live at the Mission until the padres were driven from it. Then General Pico gave him a small tract of fertile land three miles to the east of the Mission, near Pacoima Creek. But the white men were driving the Indians from their possessions, and one day Rojerio and his family, with all their belongings, were forced into a wagon, and taken away and dumped on the San Fernando county road. That night it rained, and the outcasts were without shelter or food. Rojerio's wife was then quite sickly, and because of the exposure she died in the road where they had been put.

Rojerio never forgot the awful wrong. He had deep disdain for Americans and their honor. He knew of the location of the mine which furnished the Mission padres the gold which made the San Fernando Mission famous for its gold plate. A short time before his death Rojerio showed to an Indian friend a large nugget of almost pure gold, saying that he would tell him of the location of the mine, if a deed were so drawn that no American could ever get possession of it.

When in 1846 the San Fernando Mission padres anticipated and feared an attack by the Americans they hurried away all the gold plate in the Mission and secretly buried it. In late years Rojerio was credited with being the only living person who knew where the valuable treasure was hidden, and he declared that

ROJERIO ROCHA,

Choir leader and violin player at San Fernando Mission, whose attainments Mrs. Jackson used in creating the character of Alessandro.

SHEEP-SKIN CHART

Chart showing place of burial of San Fernando Mission gold plate, made by the Fathers of that Mission with a hot sharp-pointed instrument on a sheep-skin. The lines and characters are too dim for photographing, and were retraced on the print in white for the production of this illustration. The gold plate was secretly hidden in anticipation of the coming of the United States soldiers into the San Fernando valley in 1846.

he was one of the persons who carried the plate from the Mission and buried it; yet he so hated the Americans because of the wrong done him by white men, that he persistently refused to disclose the place where the golden treasure was secreted.

A few weeks before his death he took from an old chest in his home a part of a sheep's hide, tanned on the inside, on which were tracings, arrows and crosses and other characters. This skin he gave to an old Indian companion, with the statement that the tracings and marks on it had been made by the Mission padres, and showed the location of the lost Mission plate, said to be of the value of not less than one million dollars.

Later this sheepskin was delivered by the Indian friend of Rojerio's, after the latter's death, to some white men, for a price paid and a promise to give a good share of the gold plate, if found. One of these men was a client of the writer, and the latter undertook, with others, the translation and deciphering of this chart. All agreed that the drawing led from the Mission buildings eastward to Pacoima cañon, thence up the creek from the base line of the mountains one mile. A marking on the skin which we interpreted to indicate a certain sycamore tree proved accurate. The tree stood on the south side of the cañon at the edge of the creek's bank. Directly across from this tree was a flat rock imbedded in the side of the cañon, which was another of the points indicated by the marks on the skin.

Distances were minutely measured. Every effort to locate the spot where the golden treasure lay was made with scientific accurateness. All agreed as to the place where digging should begin. The utmost secrecy was attempted. The work of uncovering the hunted gold began. Watchers were stationed up and down the cañon.

The first work was in sinking a shaft to a depth of twenty feet, as indicated by the sheepskin chart. Then a drift was cut to the west, as indicated by the drawings on the skin. Day after day, and often at night, the work progressed.

Two strangers appeared on the scene, declaring that they knew the men there were hunting for the buried plate belonging to the San Fernando Mission, and if the gold were found the Church would claim it. The lawyers advised continuing the work, and if the treasure should be found then to meet the demand of the Church, if any.

When what the expert ground men declared to have been an old tunnel was encountered in running the drift from the bottom of the twenty-foot shaft, there was great consternation and hope. All were enthused. Night shifts were put on. They dug and dug on, but in vain.

Hope died, and the attempt to find the golden plate with the aid of Rojerio's sheepskin was abandoned.

This identical sheepskin is in the possession of one of the authors.

Señora de Coronel relates and vouches for the correctness of the following story of Rojerio, which he told her and her husband with tears and sobs. He went to them as the refuge and helper of the troubled Indian.

Pacoima Creek, which empties into San Fernando valley near the town of that name, was swollen and filled with a torrent of water. The white men, who had taken his land and resented his remonstrance, tied Rojerio's hands behind him, fastened a rope around his waist, securing the other end to a rock, then threw him into the creek, and left him to what seemed certain death.

Rojerio was swiftly carried to the length of the rope, and then into a sycamore tree, to the branches of which he desperately clung for a day and a night, when the water in the swollen stream subsided and he managed to free his hands and escape.

Rojerio died in 1904 at an age supposed to have been near one hundred years. He was a giant in stature, and a Hercules in strength. A century of years did not bend his form. He was "as straight as an Indian" to the time of his death.

The life of this Indian must have impressed Mrs. Jackson, and his accomplishments and sufferings doubtless suggested some of the features and experiences of Alessandro. An Indian who could sing well and play the violin entertainingly was a rarity. Rojerio is the only one possessing such accomplishments of whom the Coronels told Mrs. Jackson, and it is a reasonable inference that the musical attainments Mrs. Jackson gave to the Indian Alessandro, the hero of her novel, were suggested by the story of Rojerio.

Mrs. Jackson was particularly interested in the sad experience of Pablo Assis, chief of the Temecula Indians. After returning to Colorado Springs she wrote to the Coronels of her intention to write a novel, "in which," quoting from the letter, "will be set forth some

THE FOUNTAIN AT CAMULOS

It is in the orange grove in front of the chapel. The railing in the center is on the south veranda of the dwelling.

GRAVEYARD AT CAHUILLA, WHERE ALESSANDRO WAS BURIED

Indian experiences in a way to move people's hearts. . . . I would like an account, written in as much detail as you remember, of the time when you, dear Mr. Coronel, went to Temecula and marked off the boundaries of the Indians' lands there. How many Indians were living there then? What crops had they? Had they a chapel? Was Pablo Assis, their chief, alive? I would like to know his whole history, life, death, and all, minutely."

Mrs. Jackson made her Alessandro the son of Pablo Assis, the Temecula Indian chief, and the sheep-shearers Temecula Indians. Pablo Assis had a son, but his name, disposition and attainments are unknown.

The experiences of Alessandro, as portrayed by Mrs. Jackson, aside from the Ramona love part, were real as to different Indians. There were the Temecula ejectment, the wanderings of members of that tribe and the killing of Juan Diego, a crazy Indian, on a spur of the San Jacinto Mountains, by Sam Temple, for horse-stealing, just as related in the story to have been the tragic death of Alessandro.

So far as can be discovered the character of Alessandro must be taken as original with Mrs. Jackson, created by her without reference to any particular person, unless it was Rojerio Rocha.

Ramona

What has been already said as to the character of Ramona may be supplemented by asserting that she was not Ramona Diego, wife of the Indian killed for horse stealing by Sam Temple, and known as Ramona Lubo, or the Cahuilla Ramona. This woman is squat, fat and unattractive. She and her baskets have been commercialized to a ridiculous extent. Susceptible tourists travel far to see her, buy the baskets she offers for sale and look upon her as the real Ramona of Mrs. Jackson's novel. Far from it.

The identity of names in this instance does not prove identity of person. "Ramona" is a common name among Indians and Mexicans. It is the feminine of "Ramon," which means the tops of branches cut for food for sheep in snowy weather. The name is beautiful and easily spoken.

In a previous chapter we have told of how Mrs. Jackson was attracted by the name "Ramona" when she first heard it, and of her declaration to the Coronels that she would use

RAMONA LUBO,

Wife of Juan Diego, killed by Jim Farrar of "Ramona," with her star basket. She is an expert basket maker and hundreds of baskets, many not made by her, have been sold as her product, and under the erroneous statement that she is the "Real Ramona."

SANTA BARBARA MISSION, FRONT VIEW

"From the west window of my room I look out on the mission (Santa Barbara) buildings. The sun rests on them from sunrise to sunset, and they seem to me to say more than any human voice on record can convey" Mrs. Jackson, *page 179.*

the name as the title to her proposed novel.

Every woman Mrs. Jackson met or heard of in California bearing the name "Ramona" is supposed to be the real Ramona of her genius. Mrs. Hartsel, of Temecula, who was Mrs. Ramona Wolfe, is accordingly, by some, declared to be the real Ramona; but she was not.

The care with which Mrs. Jackson selected the names for her characters is evidenced by a letter from her to Señor and Señora de Coronel containing the following: "I am still at work on my story ('Ramona'). It is more than half done. I wish you would ask those Indian women who made the lace for me what would be, in their Pala or San Luis Rey dialect, the words for Blue Eyes. I want to have a little child called by that name in my story, if the Indian name is not too harsh to the ear."

The "little child" proved to be the first-born of Alessandro and Ramona. It had blue eyes, a natural repetition of the eyes of Ramona's paternal Scotch ancestors. The child was named "Eyes of the Sky," but the Indian word is not given in the novel. It is related, however, that at the baptismal, "when Father Gaspara took the little one in his arms, and made the sign of the cross on her brow, he pronounced with some difficulty the syllables of the Indian name, which meant 'Blue Eyes,' or 'Eyes of the Sky.'"

When asked concerning this incident Señora de Coronel said: "I remember Mrs. Jackson's letter asking for the Indian name for 'Blue Eyes.' My husband answered it. He knew the name and gave it to Mrs. Jackson. I cannot now recall it. It is a peculiar name."

The selection of the names of two of the helpers at Camulos ranch and Felipe, the eldest son of Señora Moreno, may be reasonably conjectured. When at San Luis Rey Mission Mrs. Jackson attended the funeral services of an old Indian woman named Margarita, whose life was told to Mrs. Jackson, and greatly interested her. Margarita was a sister of Manuelito, a famous chief of several bands of the San Luisenos. Mrs. Jackson went ten miles from San Luis Rey Mission to the home of this old woman, at Potrero, passing the night there. The name Margarita she gave to "the youngest and prettiest of the maids" at Camulos.

Mrs. Jackson attended a sheep-shearing at La Puente ranch, a part of the late "Lucky" Baldwin's estate, and thus describes an incident of the occasion: "As soon as the shearers perceived that their pictures were being drawn by

SAN BUENAVENTURA MISSION, BETWEEN CAMULOS RANCH AND SANTA BARBARA

Here Father Salvierderra often officiated.

SANTA BARBARA MISSION

the artist in our party, they were all agog; by twos and threes they left their work and crowded around the carriage, peering, commenting, asking to have their portraits taken, quizzing those whose features they recognized. All were ready to pose and stand, even in the most difficult attitudes, as long as was required. Those who had done so asked, like children, if their names could not be put in the book; so I wrote them all down: 'Juan Canero, Juan Rivera, Felipe Ybara, José Jesus Lopez, and Domingo Garcia.'"

Here is evidenced her knowledge of the name Felipe. Juan Canero could have reasonably suggested Juan Canito, the name of the head-shepherd at Camulos.

Father Salvierderra

The noble character given to Father Salvierderra by Mrs. Jackson is not overdrawn. There were many of the Franciscan Fathers who lived the pure, sweet, unselfish life portrayed of this priest in "Ramona."

There was an original of Father Salvierderra. The statement of this fact by Mr. Henry Sandham, the artist, should be conclusive. He bore a commission from the

"Century Magazine" to accompany Mrs. Jackson on her California travels. It is his work that adorns Little, Brown & Company's edition of "Ramona," 1900. One of the paintings from which the illustrations are taken is the original of Father Salvierderra.

Mr. Sandham thus refers to his work with Mrs. Jackson: "At the time of the California sojourn I knew neither the name nor the exact details of the proposed book; but I did know that the general plan was a defense of the Mission Indians, together with a plea for the preservation of the Mission buildings, and so on; the whole to be enveloped in the mystery and poetry of romance. I had thus sufficient knowledge of the spirit of the text to work with keener zest upon the sketches for the illustrations; sketches which, it may be of interest to know, were always made on the spot, with Mrs. Jackson close at hand, suggesting emphasis to this object or prominence to that, as it was to have special mention in the book. . . . As for the characters themselves, I have now in my possession sketches and studies made from life at the time of my meeting the originals—a meeting that was often as much fraught with meaning for me as it was for Mrs. Jackson. . . . As illustrative of the author's fidelity to truth in character drawing, I shall mention but one of the many real characters; namely, the original of Father Salvierderra. This character is positively startling in its accurateness. I knew the original Father well, and often sought his assistance and advice. I remember I needed him once while at work in the Santa Barbara Mission, and failing to find him in any other of his favorite haunts, I entered the church, where I found him kneeling before the altar praying. He looked up as I entered, and with his usual lovable smile, said: 'I will be with you in a few minutes, my son.' Shortly he arose to his feet, threw his arm around my neck, and leaning on my shoulder (he was then well past seventy years of age) he asked as we passed down the corridor, 'What can I do to help you?' In this question lay the keynote of his whole life. At another time, as we walked through the garden, he stooped, and putting his hand under one of the gorgeous California poppies, remarked, as he turned its face up to me, 'Is not our little brother beautiful?' . . . In my studio I have the venerable Father's complete costume, given me at the time I was making the 'Ramona' sketches; it includes the cassock, cowl, sandals and hempen girdle with its symbolical five knots. The sandals are well worn and the cowl bleached and faded by the sun—marks of the endless round of toils and duties so faithfully described by Mrs. Jackson."

The omission by Mr. Sandham of the true name of the original of Father Salvierderra left the identity of that person in doubt. But the authors labored unceasingly to identify the original and with success.

The fact that the original was one of the Fathers at Old Mission, Santa Barbara, did not give certainty to the labor of discovery; for there have been, as there now are, many saintly characters within the confines of that Mission whose devout and unselfish lives have been a part of the work and history of the Catholic Church in Southern California.

Father Joseph J. O'Keefe, of Old Mission, Santa Barbara, was suggested to the authors as the original of Father Salvierderra. This thought gave a lead to the real Father Salvierderra of "Ramona." He was not Father O'Keefe, but he died in the arms of this noble and venerable Franciscan, who yet lives, and, though feeble, is still in active service at St. Francis' Orphanage, Watsonville, California.

We may positively and correctly assert that the original of Father Salvierderra was Fr.

SAN BUENAVENTURA MISSION, INTERIOR VIEW

F. Fran.co de Jesus Sanchez O. S. F.

Father Francisco de Jesus Sanchez, O. S. F., Old Mission Santa Barbara, the original of Father Salvierderra of "Ramona." "His benevolent face is well known throughout the country * * * He gives away garment after garment, leaving himself without protection against cold. * * * He often kneels from midnight to dawn on the stone floor of the church, praying and chanting psalms." (Mrs. Jackson in "*Glimpses of California and the Missions.*")

Francisco de Jesus Sanchez, O.F.M., of the Santa Barbara Mission. The records and traditions of this Mission, and evidence from other sources, establish this fact.

The Rev. Father Conradine Wallbraun, of the Old Mission, Santa Barbara, answering a letter the authors wrote to the Rev. Father Guardian of that Mission concerning the original of Father Salvierderra, says in part: "The Rev. Fr. Guardian of our Mission has authorized me to give you the desired information about the noble character, Rev. Father Salvierderra, in 'Ramona.' The hero is Rev. Fr. Francisco Sanchez, O.F.M., who died here in the Old Mission in 1884, at the side of Rev. Fr. J. O'Keefe, O.F.M., who is still living at our establishment in Watsonville, California, St. Francis' Orphanage. The Rev. Fr. O'Keefe, O.F.M., was then not well past seventy, since he was born in 1843. The death of Fr. Francisco Sanchez is well described by Mrs. Helen Hunt Jackson. Fr. O'Keefe, in whose arms the saintly Father expired, can testify to it."

At the request of the authors Father O'Keefe has written of Father Francisco Sanchez and his death expressly for this volume, and the article is here given in full:

"Many are the incidents that could be related about the Reverend Father de Jesus Sanchez, O.F.M., regarding his great missionary zeal and unbounded charity to all, his self-denial and patience in suffering. I am sorry I am so disabled, owing to the condition of my sight, which is very poor, leaving me unable to write much, and having no one who could spare the time to write at my dictation, I must be content to write what I can at present, and that is little.

"I became acquainted with the Reverend Father Sanchez in July, 1860. He was then Master of Novices at the Old Mission at Santa Barbara. He was very much sought after by pastors throughout the State to preach and give mission to the Mexican and Spanish people, and also to the Indians. So he was well known by all the ranch owners from Sacramento to San Diego, and nearly all the Spanish and Mexican people in the State knew him.

"In 1872 he was assigned to reside in the Orphanage, give missions and collect for the orphans.

"In 1882 he received several injuries. He never said much about the injuries, but bore them very patiently.

"Shortly after this he left the Orphanage

and returned to Santa Barbara, and there his injuries were aggravated by his falling over a large cut stone. A few days after he felt unable to go about much, and the doctor ordered him to be quiet and remain in his room, where he was nursed, receiving the best care and attention possible.

"I visited him often every day, and my first visit was always early every morning. The last morning I saw him very early before I went to the Church, and found him in very good humor, and seemingly very lively; so I told him I would return again as soon as I was through in the Church.

"I came as I promised, and found him lying on the bare floor, and seemingly in great pain. I raised him into a sitting posture and held him awaiting a chance to put him on the bed; but while I held him, believing he would be rested by my holding him, he gave a deep sigh and expired in my arms.

"His death occurred in 1884.

Very sincerely yours
F. Jos. J. O'Keefe O.F.M.

August 10th, 1913.
Watsonville, California."

In "Ramona" the death of Father Salvierderra is thus described: "When Father Gaspara was taking leave, Ramona said, with quivering lips: 'Father, if there is anything you know of Father Salvierderra's last hours, I would be grateful to you for telling me.'

"'I heard very little,' replied the Father, 'except that he had been feeble for some weeks; yet he would persist in spending most of the night kneeling on the stone floor in the Church, praying.'

"'Yes,' interrupted Ramona; 'that he always did.'

"'And the last morning,' continued the Father, 'the Brothers found him there, still kneeling on the stone floor, but quite powerless to move; and they lifted him, and carried him to his room, and there they found, to their horror, that he had no bed; he had lain on the stones; and then they took him to the Superior's own room, and laid him in the bed, and he did not speak any more; and at noon he died.'"

At the time of the death of Father Sanchez Mrs. Jackson was in New York writing "Ramona." The news of his death was communicated to her there, and in time for the portrayal of the dying of Father Salvierderra and the relation of the sad occurrence to Ramona by Father Gaspara of San Diego while on a visit

THE HOME OF FATHER GASPARA, SAN DIEGO

"Father Gaspara's house was at the end of a long, adobe building; but was now fallen into decay." "*Ramona.*"

THE PRIESTS' GARDEN, SANTA BARBARA MISSION

at San Pasquale, where Alessandro and Ramona had established a home, in which they made Father Gaspara their guest. He was the same Father who had married this wandering couple two years previous.

It was the custom of Father Sanchez to spend much of each day kneeling in prayer on the stone floor of the Church.

Mrs. Jackson evidently heard just sufficient of the circumstances of the death of Father Sanchez to suggest the conditions which she described as attending the death of Father Salvierderra.

Father Sanchez was in every respect the noble and saintly priest as portrayed by Mrs. Jackson in the character of Father Salvierderra.

In discovering and identifying the original of Father Salvierderra of "Ramona," the authors have been given valuable assistance by Father Theodore Arentz, O.F.M., Superior of Old Mission, Santa Barbara. We here submit an interesting communication from him upon the subject:

"I have glanced over the book 'Ramona' of Mrs. Helen Hunt Jackson, and I must say that, from what she writes about Father 'Salvierderra,' from the mention she makes of one other Father who was with him at Santa Barbara, and of other conditions and circumstances, it appears evident to me, that by Father Salvierderra she can mean no one else but Rev. Father Francisco Sanchez of the Mission Santa Barbara.

"Father Francisco Sanchez was at the time Mrs. Jackson was in Southern California (1882-83) nearly 70 years of age, he having been born in Leon, State of Guanajuato, Mexico, in August, 1813. In February, 1837, he received the habit of the Franciscan Order in the Franciscan Colegio Apostolico de Guadalupe, near Zacatecas, and in 1838 he was ordained priest. In 1841 he came with Rt. Rev. Francisco Garcia Diego y Moreno, first bishop of both Californias, who was of the same Colegio Apostolico de Guadalupe, to California, arriving at San Diego on December 11, 1841, and at Santa Barbara on January 11, 1842.

"From then on he traveled as missionary more than once over nearly all California, visiting many places frequently, and being at intervals stationed at different places, such as at San Buenaventura, 1842-43, 1852-53; at Santa Ines, 1844-50, as Vice-Rector of the seminary at Pajaro Valley Orphanage, 1874-

79, being most of the time on collection trips for the orphanage and giving at the same time missions in the different places he visited. The rest of the time he was stationed at Santa Barbara, where he held the office of Master of Novices, and from where he visited as missionary other places near and far, being invited by people and priests.

"He was a very pious and zealous padre. He died at the Old Mission, Santa Barbara, in one of the lower rooms facing the front corridor, on April 17, 1884, at 7:45 A.M., in the arms of Rev. Father Joseph O'Keefe, at the age of 70 years and 8 months.

"At about the same time Mrs. Jackson finished her book 'Ramona' in New York. Perhaps she had heard of the severe illness, or even death, of Father Francisco Sanchez at the time she finished her book.

"The young Brazilian monk, Father Francis, to whom, Mrs. Jackson says (Chap. XXV), Father Salvierderra was greatly attached, must have been Father Francisco Arbondin. He came as a young man (student) from South America, was received into the Franciscan Order at Santa Barbara on April 26, 1876, took the solemn vows May 6, 1880, and was ordained priest that same year in the month of July. In 1885 he went, with the permission of his superiors, to Guatemala.

"The Santa Barbara Mission was, according to Mrs. Jackson, the place where Father Salvierderra made his home, and here it was where Father Sanchez lived, especially after 1879, though while stationed at the Pajaro Valley Orphanage he was frequently at Santa Barbara, and from where he made his visits to different places, rancherias, etc., to give the people a chance to assist at Holy Mass, to hear the word of God preached to them, to go to confession, to receive holy communion, etc. Here, at Santa Barbara, the people also came to him.

"In her book Mrs. Jackson calls the Mission Santa Barbara promiscuously 'Franciscan Monastery' (Chap. IV), and 'College' (Chap. XXV). The Mission at that time was not a monastery in the proper sense; such it became in 1885, when it was incorporated into the Franciscan Province of the Sacred Heart of Jesus, whose headquarters are at St. Louis, Mo. Nor was it any longer a college in the common sense, or an institution of learning for young boys and men, as it had been from 1868 to 1876, when it was closed, because the Fathers were too few and too old and the hir-

VIEW FROM SANTA BARBARA MISSION TOWER

"The right tower of the Mission Church at Santa Barbara had just been completed, and it was arranged that the consecration of this tower should take place at the time of her (Señora Moreno's) wedding." "*Ramona.*"

FATHERS AND LAY BROTHERS

The eight Fathers and Lay Brothers, Old Mission, Santa Barbara, 1883, at the time of Mrs. Jackson's visit there. From left to right Fathers Francisco R. Arbondin, Bonaventura Fox, Joseph J O'Keefe, José Maria Romo, Francisco de Jesus Sanchez, Brothers Anthony Gallagher, Joseph Patrick O'Malley, Dominie C. Reid. "The Santa Barbara Mission is still in the charge of Franciscans, * * * and

ing of professors was too expensive to keep it up; but it was a missionary college, i.e., a colegio apostolico de propaganda fide, like the colegios in Mexico, from which the missionaries had come to California; though, for certain reasons, on a very small scale. As such it had been established in 1854, and such it remained until 1885.

"The community from 1880 to 1884 consisted of the following solemnly professed Fathers (priests) and Lay Brothers: Very Rev. José Maria Romo, O.F.M., Guardian Superior; Rev. Joseph J. O'Keefe, O.F.M., Vicar; Rev. Francisco Sanchez, O.F.M.; Rev. José Godiol, O.F.M.; Rev. Bonaventura Fox, O.F.M.; Rev. Francisco Arbondin, O.F.M.; Bro. Anthony Gallagher, O.F.M.; Bro. Joseph Patrick O'Malley, O.F.M.; Bro. Dominie Reid, O.F.M.

"We have a good photograph here which was taken in 1882 or 1883, and on which all the above mentioned Fathers and Brothers, except Father José Godiol, are represented.

"As to the name 'Salvierderra' used by Mrs. Jackson, I think, and I have also heard the same opinion expressed by others, that she took and changed it from 'Zalvidea,' the name of a Franciscan missionary who came to California in August, 1805, and was successively stationed at San Fernando 1805-6, at San Gabriel 1806-26, at San Juan Capistrano 1826-42, and at San Luis Rey 1842-46, when and where he died at an age of about 66 years, and who was a model missionary, and considered and much talked of by the common people as a saint; as also Bancroft remarks. Probably Mrs. Jackson heard his name mentioned when in California. Or she may have changed the name from 'Salvatierra,' the great Jesuit missionary, or apostle of Lower California, from 1697-1717.

Sincerely yours,
Theodore Arentz, O.F.M., Superior

"Santa Barbara, California,
September 4, 1913."

In "Glimpses of California and the Missions" Mrs. Jackson thus pictured Father Sanchez and the Santa Barbara Mission:

"The Santa Barbara Mission is still in the charge of Franciscans, the only one remaining in their possession. It is now called a college for apostolic missionary work, and there are living within its walls eight members of the order. One of them is very old,—a friar of the ancient *régime;* his benevolent face is well known throughout the country, and there are in many a town and remote hamlet men and women who wait always for his coming before they will make confession. He is like Saint Francis's first followers: the obligations of poverty and charity still hold to him the literal fullness of the original bond. He gives away garment after garment, leaving himself without protection against cold; and the brothers are forced to lock up and hide from him all provisions, or he would leave the house bare of food. He often kneels from midnight to dawn on the stone floor of the church, praying and chanting psalms; and when a terrible epidemic of smallpox broke out some years ago, he labored day and night, nursing the worst victims of it, shrouding them and burying them with his own hands. He is past eighty and has not much longer to stay. He has outlived many things beside his own prime; the day of the sort of faith and work to which his spirit is attuned has passed by forever.

"The Mission buildings stand on high ground, three miles from the beach, west of the town and above it, looking to the sea. In the morning the sun's first rays flash full on its front, and at evening they linger late on its western wall. It is an inalienable benediction to the place. The longer one stays there the more he is aware of the influence on his soul, as well as of the importance in the landscape of the benign and stately edifice.

"On the corridor of the inner court hangs a bell which is rung for the hours of the daily offices and secular duties. It is also struck whenever a friar dies, to announce that all is over. It is the duty of the brother who has watched the last breath of the dying one to go immediately and strike this bell. Its sad note has echoed many times through the corridors. One of the brothers said last year: 'The first time I rang that bell to announce a death, there were fifteen of us left. Now there are only eight.'

"The sentence itself fell on my ear like the note of a passing-bell. It seems a not unfitting last word to this slight and fragmentary sketch of the labors of the Franciscan Order in California."

The authors have sought to discover the origin of the name "Salvierderra." Some have accepted Padre José Maria de Zalvidea, for years one of the Fathers at San Gabriel Mission, as the original of Father Salvierderra, but merely because of some similarity of names. But not so. There is nothing in "Ramona" that in any way identifies the San Gabriel Father with Father Salvierderra of the story.

Mrs. Jackson did nothing in a light or insignificant way. She wanted a fictitious name for dear old Father Sanchez. She frequently had Señor and Señora de Coronel define and translate Spanish words and expressions for her. A superficial answer was not sufficient; she wanted the derivation of words, and often the conversation upon such a topic would lead to a lesson in etymology.

Mrs. Jackson was an intense admirer of Father Sanchez. He and Father Junipero Serra were to her almost Christ-like. She extolled their virtues, recounted with tearful sympathy their struggles and sufferings and proclaimed their lives to have been divinely perfect. She knew that the prototype of the priestly character of her proposed novel was teaching and giving salvation to his fellow-beings. She sought a name bearing significance. She had only to take the Spanish verbs *salvar,* to save, and *dar,* to give, and create the name she desired. Dropping the "r" from *salvar,* and combining the root with the subjunctive imperfect of the irregular verb *dar,* which is *diera,* produces *Salvadiera,* signifying giving salvation.

It is true Mrs. Jackson did not follow the correct Spanish spelling of the name. This may have been intentional or an error. The same comment may be made concerning the name "Alessandro." As to it Mrs. Jackson rejected the Spanish spelling, "Alejandro," and adopted the Italian.

However this may be, we find in Father Francisco de Jesus Sanchez, O.F.M., Master of Novices at Old Mission, Santa Barbara, the worthy original of Father Salvierderra of "Ramona."

Angus Phail—Ramona's Father

As further evidence of the assertion that many of the characters of the Ramona romance had their originals, is the assured fact that Angus Phail, Ramona's father, was in reality Hugo Reid, a well-known Scotchman of many eccentricities, who lived for years at San Gabriel.

Angus Phail loved Ramona Gonzaga, sister of Señora Moreno. His love was unrequited, and this drove him to desperation. "He was the owner of the richest line of ships which traded along the coast at that time. The richest stuffs, carvings, woods, pearls and jewels,

UNFINISHED CHURCH, SAN DIEGO MISSION

Brick walls of unfinished church, San Diego Mission, commenced July 16, 1869, to commemorate the one-hundredth anniversary of the founding of this Mission, as they appeared in 1913. The building is to be completed by Father Jos. Mesney work to begin January, 1914. "A few paces ... (Father Gaspara's) door stood the just begun walls of a fine brick church, which it

THE OUTER CORRIDOR, SANTA BARBARA MISSION

"When he (Felipe) rode up to Santa Barbara Mission the first figure he

which came into the country, came in his ships. . . . The Señorita Ramona Gonzaga sailed for Monterey the same day and hour her lover sailed for San Blas. . . . This was to be his last voyage. . . . He comforted himself by thinking that he would bring back for his bride . . . treasures of all sorts."

Angus returned from this last voyage to find his señorita married to an Ortegna. This maddened him. "He sold all he possessed; ship after ship sold for a song, and the proceeds squandered in drinking or worse. . . . Finally Angus disappeared, and after a time the news came up from Los Angeles that he was there, had gone out to San Gabriel Mission, and was living with the Indians. Some years later came the still more surprising news that he had married a squaw."

Ramona, as related in the story, was the child of this marriage. When a babe, Angus Phail, her father, gave her to the object of his early devotion, Ramona Gonzaga Ortegna, who was childless.

Soon afterward Angus died, and to the foster-mother of Ramona, Señora Ortegna, came an Indian messenger from San Gabriel, bearing a box and a letter, given him by Angus the day before his death. "The box contained jewels of value, of fashions a quarter of a century old. They were the jewels which Angus had bought for his bride." The note read: "I send you all I have to leave my daughter. I meant to bring them myself this year. I wished to kiss your hands and hers once more. But I am dying. Farewell."

Thus Mrs. Jackson laid the origin of the Ramona jewels.

"After these jewels were in her possession, Señora Ortegna rested not until she had persuaded Señora Moreno to journey to Monterey, and put the box into her keeping as a sacred trust. She also won from her a solemn promise that at her own death she would adopt the little Ramona. . . . One hour after the funeral . . . Señora Moreno, leading the little four-year-old Ramona by the hand, left the house, and early the next morning set sail for home."

Hugo Reid, whom we assert to be the original of Angus Phail, passed a part of his early life in Mexico, and there had an affair of the heart that shaped his future. In 1834, when twenty-three years old, he went to Los Angeles and became a merchant. He married an Indian woman at San Gabriel, Doña Victoria, said to have possessed both good looks and wealth. Of this marriage three children were born, one of them, a daughter, famed for intelligence and beauty. Her name was Ignacia, but she was commonly called "Nacha," or "Nachita." The Coronels told Mrs. Jackson the story of Hugo Reid, his marriage to the Indian woman, and of Ignacia, and she became so much interested in the facts that she planned to write another story, similar to that of "Ramona," and entitle it "Nacha."

Hugo Reid at one time was a ship-captain. He was the owner of the Esmeralda, burned at San Pedro in 1842. He brought home from ocean voyages many costly and beautiful things—diamonds, strings of pearls, silks and shawls. He had been jilted in Mexico, and left there with the avowal to marry someone bearing the name of the woman to whom he was a victim, Victoria; "even though she be an Indian," he said.

He possessed fine literary tastes, and made the Indians a special study, upon which subject he wrote extensively, his writings gaining circulation in the East and attracting general attention. There is now in the possession of Miss Annie B. Picher, Pasadena, an extensive manuscript of Hugo Reid upon the Mission Indians, of great interest, which has never been published.

A letter from Mrs. Jackson to Señor and Señora de Coronel, written at Boston, contains this reference to the original of Angus Phail: "The Hugo Reid letters I saw at the Bancroft Library, though I did not find much in them which I could use in my very limited space."

Thus is evidenced how Mrs. Jackson founded her story of "Ramona" on living persons and real facts. The Ramona jewels and silks did exist, but they were not the gems and rich fabrics of Hugo Reid. As heretofore related in these pages, they were the identical treasures of great beauty and value collected by Captain U. Yndart, a sea-faring man, of Santa Barbara, grandfather of Blanca Yndart, who, with the jewels, at the death of her mother, was given into the keeping of Doña Ysabel del Valle, mistress of Camulos ranch. This beautiful and intelligent girl was to Mrs. Jackson the inspiration of her "Ramona."

The Ranch Servants

At the time of Mrs. Jackson's visit to Camulos ranch there were such a number of house and ranch servants, of varied ages, types and

DOOR LEADING TO GRAVEYARD, SANTA BARBARA MISSION

GRAVEYARD AT SANTA BARBARA MISSION

characteristics, that numerous characters could have been readily selected by the author. Naturally she gave to them fictitious names.

There was a head shepherd, Juan Canito, an upper herdsman of the cattle, Juan José, and Luigo, "the lazy shepherd." And there were the house servants: Margarita, the "youngest and prettiest of the maids," her mother, Marda, the old cook, Anita and Maria, twins, Rosa, and Anita "the little," and Juanita, oldest of the house servants, "silly, good for nothing except to shell beans."

There were a number of shepherd dogs on the ranch, any one of which could have been identified as Capitan, Juan Canito's favorite collie, the same that followed Alessandro and Ramona in their wanderings.

Mrs. Hartsel

On departing from Camulos ranch Alessandro and Ramona directed their journey to Temecula, Alessandro's old home. The Indians had but recently been ejected from that village, and Alessandro's father, Chief Pablo Assis, was dead. There remained only ruin and devastation to mark the site of the Indian settlement, save Alessandro's home, and several others, too good for the white invaders to destroy, and Hartsel's store. The rare violin of Alessandro's father had been placed with Mrs. Hartsel for safe keeping. Alessandro planned to see her and secure money from its sale. He had his own violin with him, through the thoughtfulness of Ramona, who took it from Felipe's room the night of her escape from Señora Moreno's. "What would life be to Alessandro without a violin?" she said.

Mrs. Hartsel was the wife of Jim Hartsel, the storekeeper at Temecula. "Hartsel's was one of those mongrel establishments to be seen nowhere except in Southern California. Half shop, half farm, half tavern, it gathered up to itself all the threads of the life of the whole region. Indians, ranchmen, travelers of all sorts, traded at Hartsel's, drank at Hartsel's, slept at Hartsel's." The description of Hartsel's store and dwelling as given in "Ramona" is true to life.

Alessandro succeeded in reaching Mrs. Hartsel's kitchen early in the night unobserved, while Ramona awaited him with the horses at the cemetery. This good woman, a friend of the Indians, who knew and admired Alessandro, readily responded to the offer to sell his father's violin. But Jim, her husband, was

HARTSEL'S STORE, TEMECULA

"Hartsel's was one of those mongrel establishments, to be seen nowhere except in Southern California, * * * a long, low adobe building." "*Ramona.*"

RUINS OF MISSION SAN ANTONIO DE PALA

drunk, and no barter could be made with him; and so Mrs. Hartsel took from her purse four five-dollar gold pieces and gave them to Alessandro as a loan, saying, "I'll give you what money you need to-night, and then, if you say so, Jim'll sell the violin to-morrow, if that man wants it, and you can pay me back."

"At Temecula, from Mrs. Hartsel, Felipe got the first true intelligence of Alessandro's movements," when he was endeavoring, after Señora Moreno's death, to locate him. Mrs. Hartsel had known nothing of Ramona, or that anyone was accompanying Alessandro when he visited her on the violin errand.

This kindly woman is one of the striking characters of "Ramona," and it is interesting to know who she really was. The question may be correctly answered: she was Ramona Wolfe, whose husband kept the "mongrel establishment," store, inn and saloon at Temecula. He was a Frenchman. His wife is said to have been a half-breed; her father French. Because she bore the name of Ramona she, too, has been accepted by many as the original of that character in the romance. Mrs. Jackson met Mrs. Wolfe at Temecula and was deeply impressed by her romantic life and her sterling worth, and especially because of her friendship for the Indians.

Father Antonio Peyri

Father Antonio Peyri was a living person. He was the devoted Franciscan who built the chapel and campanile at San Luis Rey Mission. He and Pablo Assis, Alessandro's father, were close friends. Alessandro is made to say: "Father Peyri was like a father to all his Indians. My father says that they would all of them lie down in a fire for him, if he had commanded it."

Father Peyri introduced the beautiful pepper tree into California, and with his own hands planted the first of these trees in the State at San Luis Rey Mission.

In her story of "Father Junipero and His Work," to be found in "Glimpses of California and the Missions," Mrs. Jackson thus wrote of Father Peyri:

"Under the new *régime* the friars suffered hardly less than the Indians. Some fled the country, unable to bear the humiliations and hardships of their positions under the control of the administrators or majors-domo, and dependent on their caprice for shelter and even

MISSION SAN ANTONIO DE PALA, INTERIOR VIEW

FATHER ANTHONY UBACH.

Father Gaspara of "Ramona," San Diego Mission, who married Alessandro and Ramona Photographed while reading service over victims of the Bennington disaster, San Diego, June, 1906. "When fresh outrages (against the Indians) were brought to his notice, he paced his room, plucked fiercely at his black beard, with ejaculations, it is to be feared, savoring more of the camp than the altar" *"Ramona."*

for food. Among this number was Father Antonio Peyri, who had been for over thirty years in charge of the splendid Mission of San Luis Rey. In 1800, two years after its founding, this Mission had 369 Indians. In 1827 it had 2,685; it owned over twenty thousand head of cattle, and nearly twenty thousand sheep. It controlled over two hundred thousand acres of land, and there were raised in its fields in one year three thousand bushels of wheat, six thousand of barley and ten thousand of corn. No other Mission had so fine a church. It was one hundred and sixty feet long, fifty wide and sixty high, with walls four feet thick. A tower at one side held a belfry for eight bells. The corridor on the opposite side had two hundred and fifty-six arches. Its gold and silver ornaments are said to have been superb.

"When Father Peyri made up his mind to leave the country, he slipped off by night to San Diego, hoping to escape without the Indians' knowledge. But, missing him in the morning, and knowing only too well what it meant, five hundred of them mounted their ponies in hot haste, and galloped all the way to San Diego, forty-five miles, to bring him back by force. They arrived just as the ship, with Father Peyri on board, was weighing anchor. Standing on the deck, with outstretched arms, he blessed them, amid their tears and loud cries. Some flung themselves into the water and swam after the ship. Four reached it, and clinging to its side, so implored to be taken that the father consented, and carried them with him to Rome, where one of them became a priest."

Father Gaspara

Father Gaspara is named in the romance as the priest at San Diego Mission who married Alessandro and Ramona. The original of this character was Father Anthony Ubach, in charge of the San Diego Mission at the time of Mrs. Jackson's visit there. He was a sincere friend to the Mission Indians, and endeared himself to Mrs. Jackson accordingly.

This good Father was born in Barcelona. He came to California in 1860, and was stationed first at San Luis Obispo. In 1868 he moved to San Diego, and located in what is now known as "Old Town." He undertook the erection of a church there, but failed, his effort being thus related by Mrs. Jackson in "Ramona": "A few paces off from his door stood the just begun walls of a fine brick church, which it had been the dream and pride of his heart to see builded and full of worshipers. This, too, had failed. . . . To build a church on the ground where Father Junipero first trod and labored would be a work to which no Catholic could be indifferent. . . . The sight of these silent walls, only a few feet high, was a sore one to Father Gaspara—a daily cross, which he did not find grow lighter as he paced up and down his veranda, year in and year out, in the balmy winter and cool summer of that magic climate."

These same brick walls, about five feet high, stand to-day just as Mrs. Jackson saw and described them.

In a letter to the Coronels, written November 8, 1883, which gave an outline of her proposed novel, "Ramona," Mrs. Jackson said: "I have written to Father Ubach and to Mr. Morse of San Diego for their reminiscences."

In "Glimpses of California and the Missions" is this incident described by Mrs. Jackson, the priest mentioned being Father Ubach: "In the winter of 1882 I visited the San Pasquale valley. I drove over from San Diego with the Catholic priest, who goes there three or four Sundays in a year to hold service in a little adobe chapel built by the Indians in the days of their prosperity. . . . The Catholic priest of San Diego is much beloved by them. He has been their friend for many years. When he goes to hold service, they gather from their various hiding-places and refuges; sometimes, on a special *fête* day, over two hundred come. But on the day I was there, the priest being a young man who was a stranger to them, only a few were present. . . . In front of the chapel, on a rough cross-beam supported by two forked posts, set awry in the ground, swung a bell bearing the date of 1770. It was one of the bells of the old San Diego Mission. Standing bareheaded, the priest rang it long and loud: he rang it several times before the leisurely groups that were plainly to be seen in doorways or on roadsides bestirred themselves to make any haste to come."

Father Ubach wore a full beard, having received papal permission for the privilege, because of throat trouble.

Aunt Ri

The dear, sweet soul, with the Tennessee vernacular, Aunt Ri, who, with Jeff Hyer, her husband, rescued Alessandro, Ramona and

MRS. JORDAN, AUNT RI OF "RAMONA"

"Shaw, Jos! You tell her I ain't any lady. Tell her everybody around here where I live calls me 'Aunt Ri.'" *"Ramona."*

SAM TEMPLE, THE "JIM FARRAR" OF "RAMONA,"

Who killed Juan Diego, and whose tragic death Mrs. Jackson gave to the end of her hero, Alessandro. "Then with a volley of oaths, * * * leaping into his saddle * * *, as he rode away, he shook his fist at Ramona, who was kneeling * * * striving to lift Alessandro's head, and to staunch the blood flowing from the ghastly wounds." *"Ramona."*

their child from the snow storm, was Mrs. Jordan. She was thoroughly familiar with the killing of Juan Diego by Sam Temple, which furnished Mrs. Jackson the information used in telling of the tragic death of Alessandro by Jim Farrar.

She knew Juan Diego, his wife, now known as Ramona Lubo, and Sam Temple. It was she who persuaded Juan Diego to remain at her place over night, because of the long journey to his home in the mountain. In the morning Sam Temple told her someone had stolen his horse, and when she saw Juan's little pony in the corral she said she'd "bet anything that Juan took it when he had a spell on."

Juan Diego and his wife had a sick child. The latter was taken to Mrs. Jordan's home, and she gave medicine to it. When it died Mrs. Jordan tore boards from her barn to make a coffin for the dead infant.

These facts were related to Mrs. Jackson by Mrs. Jordan, as well as by Miss Sheriff, the Indian school teacher, now Mrs. Fowler, and are made a striking part of the "Ramona" story.

Jim Farrar

In a former chapter has been related the facts attending the brutal murder of a "locoed" Indian, named Juan Diego, by Sam Temple, whose horse the Indian had taken from a corral at San Jacinto. This tragedy was first given to the public by Mrs. Jackson in her "Century of Dishonor," and constituted a part of her report upon the Mission Indians to the Interior Department.

The death of Alessandro, as portrayed in "Ramona," was under the identical circumstances attending the murder of Juan Diego. It was this tragedy that gave to Mrs. Jackson the facts which she used in describing the death of her hero, Alessandro.

Sam Temple, the murderer, was the Jim Farrar of "Ramona." He never denied killing the Indian but asserted that he did it in self-defense. The story as substantially told by him was, that when he missed one of his finest horses, a beautiful black, from the corral at Hewett's, in San Jacinto, he concluded that it had been taken by an Indian; that he borrowed a shotgun, loaded both barrels with buckshot, and in addition took with him a six-shooter; that he followed the tracks of the missing horse up the mountains, riding nearly all day, when he arrived at the home of Juan Diego, and there found his horse tied to a tree; that he alighted from his horse, when Juan's wife appeared and asked what he wanted; that he told her he had come for his horse, when Juan appeared at the door; that he inquired of the Indian where he had gotten the horse, and the answer was, "at Señor Hewett's corral"; that he asked the Indian if he did not know that the horse was not his, to which the Indian replied, "yes"; that during the conversation he and the Indian were approaching each other, when suddenly the Indian drew a long-bladed knife; that he told the Indian to stop, when the latter made a lunge at him, and thereupon he pulled both triggers of his gun as it rested on his arm; that he afterwards found that he had put sixty-seven buckshot clear through the Indian, but it did not stop him at the moment, as the Indian still struck at him; that he used his gun as a club, breaking the stock on the Indian's head, who fell to the ground, but that such was the Indian's determination that even then he struck at Temple several times with the knife; that then, he, Temple, shot at the Indian three times with his revolver.

Temple was released on his preliminary hearing before a justice of the peace, and there his prosecution for the brutal crime ended.

Temple never evinced the least regret because of his dastardly act, but boasted that he had rid the country of a dangerous horse thief. He was so elated over his crime and its publication in "Ramona" that he endeavored to secure financial assistance, that he might place himself on public exhibition, as "the man who killed Alessandro."

Temple was also a wife-beater. His wife had complained to the city marshal of San Jacinto as to her husband's brutal treatment of her, and the marshal warned him not to repeat the offense; but Sam again abused his wife shamefully, her cries arousing the neighbors, who sent for the marshal. The marshal sent a deputy, a Kentuckian, who for many years had been a Pinkerton detective, with instructions to arrest Temple. It was at night when the constable approached Temple's house, and Sam called out to know who was there. He had already sent word to the marshal that he would not be taken alive and would shoot anyone who attempted to arrest him. McKim, the constable, said, "It is me, Sam. I have got to arrest you and I am going to take you dead or alive." Instantly there was a shot from Temple's revolver, which was without effect. Quick as a flash the constable returned the shot, striking Sam's arm and badly injuring it. Immediately Sam yelled out that he had had enough. The constable ordered him to throw out his gun and to stand clear in the light, and throw up his hands. The order was obeyed. McKim took Sam to the jail, had his arm bandaged and locked him up.

Temple last lived at Yuma, Arizona, where he died in 1909.

Judge Wells

Judge Tripp, the justice of the peace at San Jacinto, before whom Sam Temple had his preliminary hearing under the charge of killing Juan Diego, is the Judge Wells of "Ramona." Mrs. Jackson thus wrote of him: "Judge Wells was a frontiersman, and by no means sentimentally inclined; but the tears stood in his eyes as he looked at the unconscious Ramona."

Judge Wells is another of the characters of "Ramona" drawn from life.

CHAPTER XIV

DOÑA MARIANA DE CORONEL—THE CORONEL COLLECTION—BISHOP AMAT—SAINT VIBIANA'S CATHEDRAL—DON ANTONIO AND GENERAL KEARNEY—LETTERS OF MRS. JACKSON TO THE CORONELS

IN 1900 Doña Mariana de Coronel, the intimate friend of Mrs. Jackson, bade farewell to Los Angeles, intending to spend her declining years in Old Mexico, which, in the days of peace and prosperity and contentment, she often had visited with Don Antonio, her husband.

As a maiden she had spent many happy years in the old pueblo that clustered about the Los Angeles Plaza, knowing everybody, known to all, beloved by everybody. Years of unalloyed bliss followed as the mistress of "El Recreo," the ideal Spanish abode that Don Antonio had builded amidst the orange trees in the broad grant made by the Mexican Government to his father and descended to him, not far from the sloping banks of the Los Angeles River, and what now would be near the corner of Seventh Street and Central Avenue; although it is

JUDGE TRIPP, JUSTICE OF THE PEACE,

Judge Wells of "Ramona," sitting, and Sam Temple, Jim Farrar of "Ramona," standing, and the building where the preliminary trial of the latter for the murder of Alessandro was held. Farrar "rode straight to * * * Judge Wells, * * * and said that he wished to surrender himself as having [illegible] on an Indian * * * who had stolen his horse." "*Ramona.*"

STATUARY WORK OF SEÑORA DE CORONEL

Part of the Coronel Collection, Chamber of Commerce, Los Angeles.

doubtful if even Doña Mariana herself could indicate the precise location of the historical hacienda, so confusing are the lines of what has by common consent come to be called "civilization."

Mixed must have been the memories that crowded in upon Doña Mariana as she withdrew from the scenes of her childhood and set her face to the southward. It had been her purpose to locate at or near Guadalajara, and there duplicate the hacienda that, as her hospitable home for so many years, had come to be so prominent a landmark in Los Angeles, a home that had sheltered every prominent person of every nationality who had visited the pueblo during Spanish, Mexican and American occupation.

Were this a history, which it is not intended to be, many chapters would need to be devoted to accounts of what Doña Mariana and her distinguished husband had done for Los Angeles. It must suffice to make reference to one of the latest generous acts of Doña Mariana, the gift to the Los Angeles Chamber of Commerce of the wonderful Coronel Collection, comprehending relics and curios she and her husband had been fifty years in assembling, and which constitute the chief attraction of the

Chamber of Commerce. Days and weeks could be profitably spent in examining this collection, the *ensemble* in itself constituting a very comprehensive history of the State of California, from the days of Junipero Serra down to the present era, and including articles associated with Helen Hunt Jackson and "Ramona."

Interest in the collection is greatly enhanced by the knowledge of the fact that many of the more interesting articles were the product of the genius and skill of Don Antonio and Doña Mariana themselves. Conspicuous among the latter are the figures of a Spanish woman and man, mounted upon gorgeously caparisoned steeds for which the State was at the time famous, both figures attired in full Spanish costumes, faithful to history, with not an item omitted. Near by is a miniature of San Luis Rey Mission building, walls and grounds, as seen before the days of secularization.

There are sketches in black and white and in oil, all of rare merit, and parchments of priceless value. Conspicuous among the curios is the little mahogany table, ordered made by Don Antonio for the special convenience and comfort of Helen Hunt Jackson in her literary work, after the unfortunate mishap that crippled her for life and made it difficult for her to write except in a reclining position.

In this collection is the first cannon brought to California, of which Mrs. Jackson thus wrote in "Glimpses of California and the Missions": "The place of honor in the room is given, as well it might be, to a small cannon, the first cannon brought into California. It was made in 1717, and was brought by Father Junipero Serra to San Diego in 1769. Afterward it was given to the San Gabriel Mission; but it still bears its old name, 'San Diego.' It is an odd little arm, only about two feet long, and requiring but six ounces of powder. Its swivel is made with a rest to set firm in the ground. It has taken many long journeys on the backs of mules, having been in great requisition in the early Mission days for the firing of salutes at festivals and feasts."

The future historian, let us hope, will do at least partial justice to the far-sighted wisdom and the broad generosity of Don Antonio and Doña Mariana in patiently assembling this unique collection, from all quarters of the globe, and at such sacrifice as no one ever will know, and presenting it as a free gift to Los Angeles, when a king's ransom would have been paid for it, had she been content with its removal hence.

Appearances are deceptive. Things are not always what they seem. Guadalajara may have been as beautiful as Doña Mariana in her mind's eye had pictured it. But travel farther into the interior satisfied her that other places, and for a variety of reasons, were more desirable as a place of ultimate residence, and when the City of Oaxaca was reached Guadalajara lost the opportunity of securing a rare acquisition.

Although remote from the capital and from centers of so-called civilization, easily one hundred and fifty miles from railway connections, Oaxaca, in the judgment of Doña Mariana, is the garden spot of the earth, to which she will joyfully return when the strife in the Republic shall have ceased.

Señora Coronel came north in August of 1912, and has been dividing her time between relatives in Los Angeles and its environs.

The land holdings of Doña Mariana in the State of Oaxaca are not measured by varas or by acres. Their hacienda is so many leagues in one direction by so many leagues in another. Poor indeed would be the landlord the limits of whose hacienda could be measured by the eye. "Oh, we know nothing about acres," said Doña Mariana. "If a man has land for sale it is so much for 'the piece,' and

DON ANTONIO DE CORONEL AND HIS WIFE, MARIANA. (*Permission of Miss Annie B Picher, Pasadena.*)

"A beautiful young Mexican woman. * * * Her clear, olive skin, soft brown eyes, delicate, sensitive nostrils, and broad, smiling mouth, are all of the Spanish Madonna type, and when her low brow is bound * * * by turban folds * * * her face becomes a picture indeed. She is the young wife of a gray-headed Mexican, Señor Don Antonio." (Mrs. Jackson in "*Glimpses of California and the Missions.*")

THE FIRST CANNON BROUGHT INTO CALIFORNIA

Don Antonio de Coronel and the first cannon in California, brought by Father Junipero Serra in 1769.

'the piece' may contain five, ten, or twenty thousand acres, as you measure land up here. The vendor is quite indifferent; he doesn't seem to care a rap whether you buy or not, unless he happens to take a fancy to the would-be purchaser. In that event the price cuts little figure; it is usually quite normal, and coupled with the condition that the buyer build near to him, his companionship appearing to be more valued than his dollars. It is a life of ease and of contentment. Human labor there is so cheap that one becomes accustomed to constant and perfect service. Where help can be obtained in abundance for ten cents a day there is not much occasion for one to exert himself physically. The peon in Mexico, like the black man in the South in ante-bellum days, is ever at hand to brush off the flies."

What is fairer than a day in June—in Southern California! On the expansive porch of "El Retrio," Covina suburban villa of Mr. C. D. Griffiths, were that gentleman and his wife, a niece of Señora de Coronel, and grand-niece Eileen; Mrs. Ellen Pollard, a sister of Señora de Coronel; Mrs. Earle, another sister, her husband and three children.

And there were Ramona and Alessandro. No, on reflection, it must be admitted those characters were not present, though it always seems as if they are when Doña Mariana is about.

Mrs. Jackson usually kept standing on her desk an unframed photograph after Dante Rossetti—two heads, a man's and a woman's, set in a nimbus of clouds, with a strange and beautiful regard and meaning in their eyes. They were exactly her idea of what Ramona and Alessandro looked like. The characters of the novel, she thought, came nearer to materialization in this photograph than in any other way.

And so with Doña Mariana. It is difficult to disassociate her from the characters she helped so much to create.

It was distinctly a home scene. Mrs. Griffiths had sent the writer this note: "My aunt wishes me to ask you and your wife to visit her here at Covina this coming Sunday. If you will let us know on what car to expect you, Mr. Griffiths will meet you at Citrus Avenue. If convenient to you, we would like to have you come and spend the day with my aunt."

It was most convenient and we spent a day the memories of which will only fade with loss of consciousness.

"How did it happen that you and the Don did not accompany Mrs. Jackson on her journey to the Indian villages?" she was asked. "It had been so arranged," she answered, "but I became too ill to go, and my husband did not feel like leaving me alone for so long a period."

Señora de Coronel told many interesting stories during the day. The one concerning Bishop Thaddeus Amat and Saint Vibiana's Cathedral in Los Angeles being of special interest, is here retold:

"It will sound more like a romance than reality," said Doña Mariana. "Bishop Thaddeus Amat was the parish priest in Los Angeles when Father Mora was Bishop of Los Angeles and Monterey. He was a good man, oh, one of the noblest of God's creatures. The spiritual welfare of his flock, the material as well as the spiritual welfare of the Indians—he thought of naught else. It was he who built Saint Vibiana's Cathedral at the corner of Second and Main streets. The building of that cathedral had been the ambition of his life. It is an interesting and a pathetic story. I am told it is the purpose soon to build another and a larger cathedral elsewhere. I suppose it will be done before long, that ground having become so valuable for business purposes; but it will be a great pity to tear it down. I shall hope never to see it done.

"Bishop Amat was a poor peasant in Italy, a sheepherder. When quite young he told his parents he had had a dream, a dream that he was a priest and had built a great cathedral to a Saint. Soon after he had the same dream, and when it was repeated the third time, his mother, thinking it a very strange circumstance, told the story to her parish priest. That worthy was much affected by the relation, and asked that the child be brought to him. He was found to be unusually intelligent, and especially informed regarding religious matters. He had improved his time while attending his sheep in reading church history, and was indeed so precocious that the priest declared he must be given greater opportunities for storing his mind with knowledge. He was sent to Rome and studied for the priesthood, and in time was ordained and sent to America. Not long after his arrival in this country he was assigned to the Los Angeles diocese.

"While serving as the parish priest here, when Bishop Mora was in charge of the diocese, Bishop Amat had occasion to visit Rome.

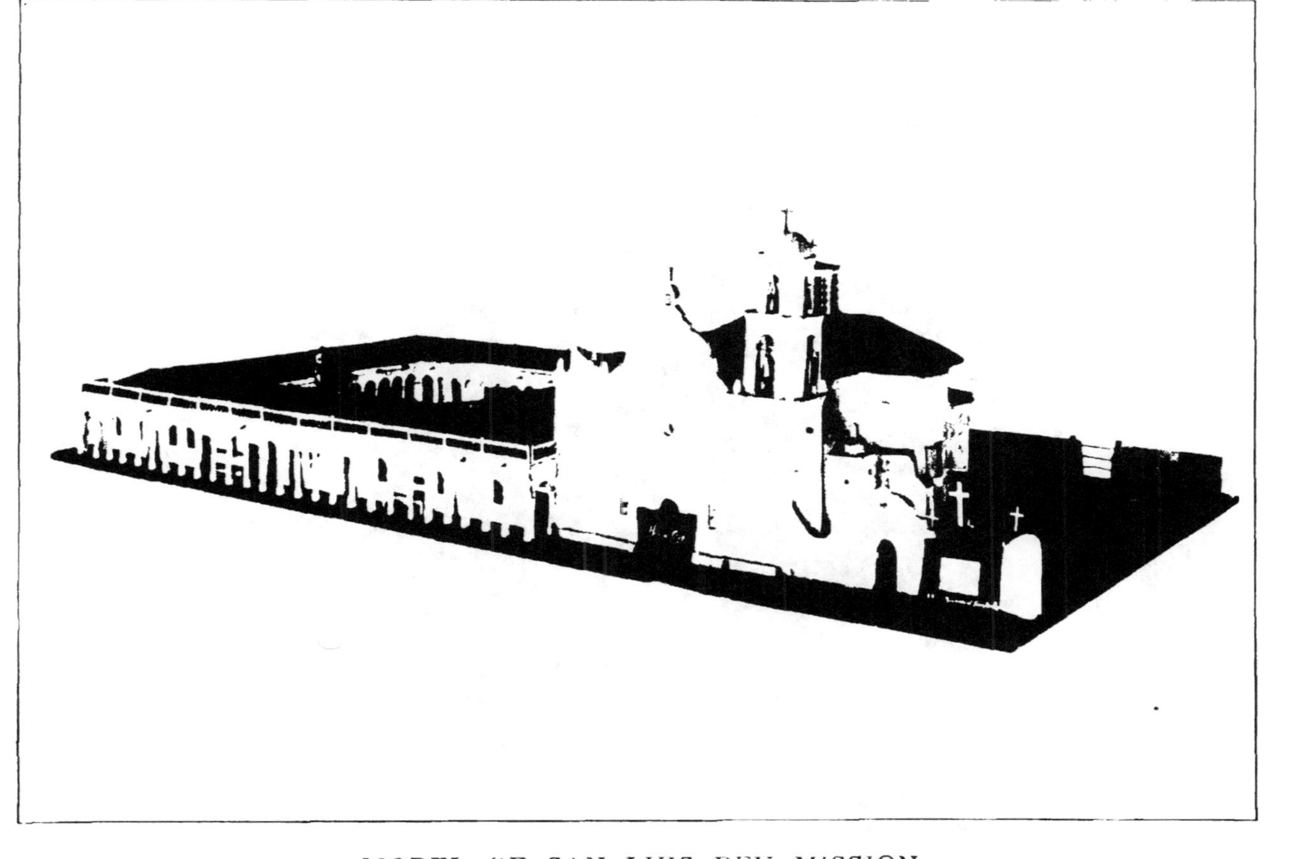

MODEL OF SAN LUIS REY MISSION

Made by Señor and Señora de Coronel, being a part of the Coronel Collection, Chamber of Commerce, Los Angeles.

FRONT VIEW OF ST VIBIANA'S CATHEDRAL,
LOS ANGELES

While there he went to the catacombs, and there witnessed the opening of the casket containing the remains of Saint Vibiana. She was a child Saint, you know, and the casket was small, bound about with brass hoops. Exposed to view the features for the moment were seen to be precisely as in life, her childish beauty in no way changed, but exposure to the air had the inevitable and almost immediate effect—everything disappeared but the bare skeleton.

"Bishop Amat was much affected by what he had seen. He begged that the skeleton of Vibiana be given to him, promising that if it were placed in his charge he would bring it to America and build a great cathedral, which would be named for the Saint and dedicated to her memory.

"Returning here he at once began the work. Large contributions were offered to him, but all these were refused. He wanted the church built with the offerings of the common people. And so it came about. The money poured in from all quarters, and soon he had enough in the treasury to warrant the building of the Cathedral of Saint Vibiana.

"In the upper part of the altar is a crypt in which are deposited the remains of the Saint, in the little brass-bound casket in which they were brought from Rome. Under the altar are the remains of Bishop Amat.

" Would it not seem sacrilege ever to remove them? When the church was dedicated Bishop Amat told the congregation that he had a story rather than a sermon to deliver, and recited the facts substantially as here given.

" After this great work was achieved Bishop Amat undertook another worthy enterprise, in the north. In the charming valley in which is situated the Carmelo Mission he secured a considerable tract of land which he intended to use as a school for Indian boys, to teach them agriculture. But before his arrangements for this were completed the sale of the land was negotiated to a syndicate of white men. Bishop Amat of course objected, and the Indians protested. The chiefs of all the Indian villages were asked to sign a certain paper. Before signing they brought it to me, and I advised them not to sign it, or any other paper without first submitting it to Don Antonio. The paper was a quit-claim to the water rights to all their lands. Had they signed the instrument their lands would have become worthless. It would have left them without a drop of water for irrigating purposes.

"Bishop Amat died in prayer. An attendant, thinking it time he should retire, gently and hesitatingly approached the old man, as, upon his prayer rug in front of the altar at the Church of Saint Vibiana, he was supposed to be counting his beads and repeating his invocations. Passing the altar, some time thereafter, he found the devoted old man still in the posture of heavenly supplication. Aged and feeble, weak and emaciated, the attendant felt the duty doubly incumbent upon him of withdrawing him hence to his chamber, for rest he so much needed. This time he was a trifle more insistent, but his solicitude was quite needless; Bishop Amat was rigid in death!"

On the slab which enclosed the crypt in which the body of Vibiana was found were these Latin words: *"Animas innocenti atque pudicae Vibiana in pace depositae pridie Kalendas Septembris";* the translation of which is, "To the innocent and chaste soul of Vibiana, whose remains were deposited in peace on the day before the Calends of September."

On the exterior of St. Vibiana's Cathedral are these letters, "D.O.M.," being the abbreviations for *"Deo Optimo Maximo,"* which means, "To God the Greatest and Best." Also the sentence, "*Dicata* A.D. 1876," signifying the date when the Cathedral was dedicated, and the words, *"Sub Invocatione Sanctae Vibianae Virginis et Martyris,"* the translation of which is, "Under the Invocation of Saint Vibiana, Virgin and Martyr."

"Don Antonio," said Doña Mariana, "was loyal to the Church, but he ever was friendly with the Indians. He had good reason for being true to them, for upon more than one occasion they had saved his life.

"Don Antonio de Coronel was one of the liberal contributors to the erection of Saint Vibiana's Cathedral, and materially aided in its construction and establishment. A special part of his donation was a number of thousands of the brick which went into the building. He was buried from this Cathedral.

"No," said Señora de Coronel, "it is not as you suppose. I am no longer attached to Los Angeles. It is not as it used to be. I am anxious to return to Mexico, where conditions are much as they were here fifty years ago. But I fear it will be a long time before normal conditions are restored. Porfirio Diaz is a much abused and a much misunderstood man. He best knew how to rule Mexico. He knew every renegade in the country, and how to handle the warring factions. I fear it will be a long time

THE ALTAR, ST VIBIANA'S CATHEDRAL, LOS ANGELES

In the niche, in the upper part, is the casket containing the remains of St. Vibiana. Under the altar are the remains of Bishop Thaddeus Amat, builder of the Cathedral.

INTERIOR OF ST VIBIANA'S CATHEDRAL, LOS ANGELES

before peace is restored. Few know the real cause of the factional division of the country. Nearly all the women in Mexico are true to the Church, while most of the men are Masons; hence the irrepressible conflict. I am glad Senator del Valle has been sent down there to harmonize the factions. He may not succeed; but he is more likely to do so than any American ambassador.

"No, I do not believe the Coronel Collection will be removed from the Chamber of Commerce. That seems to be the best place for it, the place where the larger number of people can conveniently see it. There was but a single condition of its gift to the city: that no item in the collection should ever be disposed of by sale, gift or otherwise. It must always be kept intact, just as it was when I turned it over to the city.

"I never met Mr. Jackson. It never seemed convenient for me to visit Mrs. Jackson at her Colorado home, although frequently beseeched to do so. I knew of her wish to be buried upon the slopes of Cheyenne Mountain. There were few things about Mrs. Jackson I did not know, for we were like sisters. When the site of her grave came to be a public picnic ground, and Mr. Jackson began to feel the necessity of removing her remains, he wrote me, asking if his wife had ever expressed a willingness to be buried elsewhere. I knew the reason for her peculiar request, and wrote to him about it, leaving him to draw his own inferences and act upon his own judgment. It was due wholly to the neglect and desecration of the grave of Junipero Serra that Mrs. Jackson decided upon a burial spot upon the mountain she loved so much. She never dreamed it would become a public resort. I was glad when I learned that she rested peacefully at Evergreen Cemetery, Colorado Springs."

Señora de Coronel has permitted the authors to read the numerous letters written by Mrs. Jackson to her and Don Antonio, her husband, and to publish the following, selected for the purpose. It will aid to understand the letters to here again state that "Ramona" was written in New York during the winter of 1883-84, and Mrs. Jackson returned to California in the latter part of 1884, went to San Francisco in April, 1885, and there died August 12th of that year.

Santa Barbara, Cal.,
January 30, 1882.

My Dear Friends, Mr. and Mrs. Coronel:

. . . I have now been one week in Santa Barbara, and am still homesick for Los Angeles. I have not as yet seen anything so fine as the San Gabriel Valley, and San Bernardino Mountains with the snows on the tops, and I have not found any one to tell me the things of the olden time so eloquently as you did.

I have seen Father Sanchez, Father O'Keefe and Father Francis, at the Mission, and have obtained from their library some books of interest. From the west window of my room I look out on the Mission buildings. The sun rests on them from sunrise to sunset, and they seem to me to say more than any human voice on record can convey. You will perhaps have heard that I was so unfortunate as not to find Mrs. del Valle at home, so I only rested two hours at her house and drove on to Santa Barbara that night. I saw some of the curious old relics, but the greater part of them were locked up, and Mrs. del Valle had the keys with her.

The most interesting part of my journey was San Fernando. There I could spend a whole day, and I must tell you of a mistake

I made; perhaps if you see Mr. Pico you can rectify it for me. He said to me, when he was showing me some of the relics they have, "Now, if you like, you can take some one of these things." Of course I desired very much to have some of them; but I replied, merely out of the wish not to seem greedy or ungrateful, "Oh, you are too kind to think of such a thing. I am afraid you ought not to give away any of them. Do you not rather prefer to keep them for the Church?" And then he did not again offer them to me, and I was all the rest of the time waiting and hoping that he would; but I came away without having the opportunity again to take anything. I suppose you wil' think I was very stupid. Indeed, I think so myself; but it is partly that I do not understand the customs of the Spanish people in regard to such things.

If it should happen that you see any of the family, you can tell them of my regret for having made such a mistake, and that I would be very glad to have anything they would like to part with. One of the old candlesticks I would very much like to have, or one of the old books of St. Augustine I had in my own mind decided that I would choose.

I also wanted very much to have a piece

FATHER JOAQUIN IN PULPIT AT SAN GABRIEL MISSION, WEARING VESTMENTS OF FATHER JUNIPERO SERRA

SAN FERNANDO MISSION

of one of the old olive trees if I could have found one that had blown down—a straight section of the trunk sawed across, about six inches thick, to make a round block, polished to set my stone bowl on. The driver promised to take two of the old palm leaves to you to keep. I thought you would like one; the wind had strewed the ground with them. But I think it rained so hard the days he went back he did not stop to look for palm leaves.

When I come again with the artist we will go to San Fernando. It is one of the places I desire to see twice.

I send you also by to-day's mail a copy of my little volume of poems. I thought that you would like that volume better than any other I have written. In a little more than four months I hope to see you again.

Truly yours, and with many thanks for all your kindness,

Helen Jackson.

San Francisco, 1600 Taylor St.,
June 27, 1885.

My Dear Friends:

I am glad to see the accounts in the papers you have sent me of some farther movements in relation to the Mission Indians, and I have been much cheered by an interview with Prof. Painter.

If he really undertakes to get something done for those Indians, he will be worth more than all the Senators and Congressmen put together.

I hope he will return to Southern California and visit the rest of the villages. He is thinking of it.

Have you yet been up the Verdugo cañon to get those two baskets I ordered from the old Indian woman there? I fear she will think me a "lying white," if she does not get the money before long.

I am sorry to tell you I am still in bed: the malarial symptoms seem to be over, but it has left me in a state of nervous prostration which nothing touches. I can eat literally nothing, and of course am very weak; it has been a trying experience and I fear I have months more of it yet to come.

It is a year to-morrow since I broke my leg! My unlucky year.

I have been asked by one of the eastern magazines (a children's magazine) to write a poem, narrating some incident or legend in California life—if possible something to do with the Indians. I do not know anything which seems to me to be adapted to tell in a ballad; and I have wondered if in Mr. Coronel's storehouse of memories he could not think of some old stories which would be suitable for the purpose. If he can and you would write them down for me I would be greatly obliged to you. I hope you are all well.

Always faithfully your friend,

Helen Jackson.

P. S. When you get those baskets I would like to have them sent by express. There is no doubt that I shall have to lie here for many weeks yet, and I shall enjoy having them. Send with them, also, the flat one I gave to you to keep. I'd like that to keep work in on my bed.

The following is the last letter written by Mrs. Jackson to the Coronels, and preceded her death just six days:

San Francisco, Calif.
1600 Taylor St.,
Aug. 6, 1885.

Dear Mr. Coronel:

When the baskets are done send them by express to this address: Mrs. Merritt Trimble, 59 E. 25th St., New York.

Send all the baskets you have.

I am failing now fast. I think I cannot live a great while.

In your letter to Mrs. Trimble tell her about the stone bowls and pestles, and ask her if she wants those too. She will write and tell you.

Goodby. With very much love to your wife and you always,

Helen Jackson.

CHAPTER XV

CONTRIBUTED BY DOÑA MARIANA DE CORONEL—HER ASSOCIATION WITH MRS. JACKSON

"YOU are going to get well, Mariana. You will survive me. I feel that you will live to complete my work." Thus said Mrs. Jackson to me but a few short weeks before her death. Often she had talked in that vein. She seemed ever to have a presentiment that I would survive her.

One of her most coveted projects, after her visit to the Indian settlements and her report to the Government, was the institution at some available place of a school for Indian women and girls, where instruction could be given in all of the useful arts, to the end that they might in time become self-sustaining. Regarding the details of this enterprise Mrs. Jackson talked frequently with my husband, Don Antonio, and myself.

"I shall endeavor to secure an appropriation from Congress for the necessary grounds, and these shall be deeded directly to the Indians," said Mrs. Jackson. "For the buildings

I shall appeal to the people of the East for donations, and I shall endeavor to have the institution abundantly endowed. But you and Don Antonio must, at whatever sacrifice, take charge of the institution and make a success of it. Congress has passed the act that you and the Don and I have drafted, providing for the granting of lands to the Indians in severalty; but little good will come of it unless these poor people are taught how to make a living for themselves aside from the weaving of baskets. Nobody but you and dear Don Antonio can successfully carry out my ideas. I am counting upon meeting with numerous obstacles in getting the Indians to give up their tribal relations. To them it will be an immense problem, a complete change in their mode of life, and we may not expect that all will adopt it cheerfully. I am counting upon the influence that you and Don Antonio can exert to reconcile them to the transformation. Indeed I should entertain all sorts of fear and apprehension and doubt regarding the outcome, but for the compelling influence which you and your husband can exert. No one else I have in mind can be intrusted with the work."

Mrs. Jackson gave much thought to the working out of the details at the California end of the line. She counted largely upon the support, financial and otherwise, that Hon. Henry M. Teller, then Secretary of the Interior, would give to her noble and highly practical enterprise. Don Antonio and I sympathized thoroughly with her, and stood ready to lend hearty assistance when required. But Mrs. Jackson's early death forever sealed the fate of the educational undertaking.

Nearly thirty years have passed since Helen Hunt Jackson put her arm lovingly about me and declared her belief that I would survive her, and that the completion of her life's work would devolve upon me. To some persons "Time's unpitying fingers" may begin "to smooth out and obliterate the lines, once so sharp and distinct, with which she engraved herself on the consciousness of her contemporaries." To some persons even her memory may have grown dim, as the impression of a face long unseen fades, until no longer can be recalled the exact look and smile. This is regarded as the inevitable law, each day bringing its "little dust our soon choked hearts to fill." But it has never been so with me. Never a day or night but I feel her presence. Once, I well remember, she said: "Mariana, if it be possible in the next world to come to you in trouble or grief or distress, you may count upon me doing so." The promise has never been forgotten. The suggestion has never once passed from my memory.

Eight months ago, at the beginning of the terrible fratricidal strife that has brought so much misery to my country and its people, I thought it best I should return to the United States before it should become too hazardous to undertake the journey. It involved a mule-back trip of one hundred and fifty miles over the mountains to the nearest railway station; not a cheerful prospect for a woman of my years to undertake. But I entered upon it with the utmost confidence that Helen Hunt Jackson would be with me every foot of the way, protecting me from every possible danger. As though in life, she seemed to place her hand upon my shoulder and assure me that all would be well.

I have never thought much about spiritualism. I am not a spiritualist. And yet, oh, so many times since, when trouble and grief have been my lot, when clouds encircled my pathway, when gloom surrounded and threatened to engulf me, I have suddenly been brought to a realization that Mrs. Jackson's

DOÑA MARIANA DE CORONEL, LOS ANGELES

Intimate friend of Helen Hunt Jackson, photographed in 1913—especially for this volume. Señora de Coronel and her husband, Don Antonio, really inspired "Ramona" and gave to its author the principal facts of the story. She is holding the copy of "Ramona" given her by Mrs. Jackson.

FIRST COPY OF "RAMONA" TRANSLATED INTO SPANISH,

Presented by the translator to Señora de Coronel.

spirit was near, that she was shielding me, that in her presence no harm could come.

My acquaintance and association with her has constituted one of the fondest and sweetest recollections of my whole life. Our meeting was singular. Had she come in any other way than she did, her first visit, it is likely, would have been her last. I had never heard of her or her books. Like most Spanish people, I shrank from publicity. Had she simply introduced herself as a correspondent of the "Century Magazine," it is likely I should have taken little interest in what she had to say. But she brought a letter from Bishop Mora to Don Antonio and myself. In it the Bishop asked us to give her all the information we could regarding the Mission Indians. This we proceeded to do, her interest in our relation of the story of their treatment, so far as had come within our observation and experience, being singularly intense.

She made an engagement to come again the following week, and it happened to be Christmas day, 1881. While she and Don Antonio and myself were seated on the veranda, at the old hacienda in the orange grove, Los Angeles, five or six Indian chiefs rode into the court, in a high state of excitement. Don Antonio excused himself from the circle and stepped out to converse with the chiefs. They were talking with great animation, and to my amazement I observed that Mrs. Jackson was following the conversation with the closest attention, although she could understand not a word of what was being said. I noticed her lips moving in unison with the voices of the chiefs, although she made no audible sound. She seemed to be repeating what they said, or endeavoring to comprehend its meaning. It was perfectly obvious that they were deeply in earnest, and finally, as if she could stand it no longer, Mrs. Jackson addressed Don Antonio and asked if she might not talk with the Indians. The request was of course promptly granted. I acted as interpreter, and soon Mrs. Jackson was in full possession of the reason for their visit.

White men had secured possession of the water rights to their land, and it was to them no better than a desert. Mrs. Jackson comprehended the whole story, and secured the consent of the Indians to visit their settlements, Don Antonio assuring them that she was their friend and would work in their interest.

She had secured the services of Mr. Abbot Kinney, and obtained his appointment as a co-commissioner soon after, and the details of the now celebrated official journey through the country of the Southern California Mission Indians were arranged at our home.

The party consisted of Mrs. Jackson, Mr. Abbot Kinney, the late Mr. Henry Sandham, the "Century's" artist, and Mr. N. H. Mitchell, the proprietor of a livery stable and hotel at Anaheim, whose two-seated carriage was used for a part of the journey, he acting as driver. This carriage was soon abandoned, however, not being suited to all purposes of the trip, and most of it was made on horseback, or rather mule-back, as the sure-footed little burros of the Indians were more suited to the condition of the trails over the mountains. Indeed, I later was advised that the party visited some places high up on the mountain sides, or on the borders of the desert, where it was possible only to go afoot. On one occasion, contemplating a hazardous journey into the mountains, I remonstrated with Mrs. Jackson and attempted to dissuade her from the trip. Her answer was, "I must see those poor Indians, and I'll go if I die."

At this time, before the journey was undertaken, Mrs. Jackson was a guest at Mrs. Kimball's boarding house on New High Street, then about the best place of entertainment in Los Angeles. Mr. Kinney and Mr. Sandham, pending completion of the arrangements, were guests at our home.

Don Antonio was a veritable encyclopedia, and was able to recall, with the slightest effort, every important event since his boyhood. His knowledge covered the whole period of Spanish, Mexican and American rule, from the time of his arrival in California until his death. His information regarding the Indians was particularly full and accurate; hence he was of invaluable assistance to Mrs. Jackson in all her work. But his knowledge of the English language was limited, and the work of interpreting fell largely upon me.

Mrs. Jackson made many notes regarding the story of "Ramona" at our home. She discussed the intended book with us on many occasions, and told us she would name it "Ramona." She would gladly have located the scene of "Ramona" at our hacienda, and doubtless would have done so but for the suggestion made by Don Antonio himself, and insisted upon by him, that Camulos was the more fitting place. We both assured her that the Camulos Rancho was one of the few remaining of the old Spanish homesteads where the original life of a California hacienda still existed. It was about the only place yet existing where the original California hacienda could still be studied in all its poetry and importance. We told her of the patrician character of Camulos. Here, we told her, might still be studied the pressing of the Mission olive in the old *morteros*, the gathering of the vintage in Hispano-Indian fashion, the making of Spanish wine, the Spanish sheep-shearing, under an Indian *capitan*; here were still the picturesque retainers; here were distinguished family traditions—all the elements, in fact, upon which the book might grow with historic fidelity.

Notwithstanding all these facts, the author might easily and with perfect fidelity to truth and tradition, have located the scenes at the Coronel hacienda. But there was another fact, another barrier, and a well-nigh insurmountable one: the excessive modesty of Don Antonio himself. So marked a characteristic of him was this that, notwithstanding all he had done for Los Angeles, notwithstanding the fact that he had labored for thirty years to clear the title to Elysian Park, that it might become the property of the city in fee simple, without a shade or shadow, he steadily declined even the small honor, so often sought to be conferred upon him, of having a street named for him.

But it is true, it is history—and it would not be history if it were not true—that the inspiration of "Ramona" was Don Franco Antonio de Coronel, my husband, under whose expansive roof it sprouted and grew, and there it was christened with the name by which it soon came to be known and ever will be known, "Ramona."

After Mrs. Jackson's return to California in 1884, the story of "Ramona" having been published, she did much writing at our home. She had broken her leg before leaving Colorado Springs by falling down the stairway in her home, and she had to write in a reclining position. Don Antonio, my husband, had a little table made especially for her use, Mrs. Jackson specifying its height, and requesting the placing of two shelves in it upon which she could lay her finished sheets or notes. Much of her writing during her stay in Los Angeles in 1884-85, was done on this table, which is now a part of the Coronel Collection in the Los Angeles Chamber of Commerce.

Mrs. Jackson selected the Camulos Rancho

FIRST COPY OF "RAMONA" AND TABLE ON WHICH MOST OF THE MANUSCRIPT WAS WRITTEN

(1) First copy of "Ramona" seen by Mrs. Jackson was at the postoffice in Los Angeles, which she presented on its receipt to Señora de Coronel.

(2) The table ordered made by Don Antonio de Coronel for Helen Hunt Jackson, and on which she did much of her writing at the Coronel home, now in the Coronel Collection,

INSCRIPTION IN FIRST COPY OF "RAMONA"

Inscription written by Helen Hunt Jackson in first copy of "Ramona" she received, and which she gave to Señora de Coronel.

as the home of Ramona. This I know, not only because of general conversations with her, but she positively declared to me that it was Camulos Rancho which she sought to describe in the story of "Ramona," and that that rancho was the home of Ramona.

In the latter part of 1884 Mrs. Jackson returned to Los Angeles. "Ramona" had not been issued from the press at the time of her departure from the East. I went with her to the postoffice one day, when a package was delivered to her there. She opened it, and there was a copy of "Ramona," the first she had seen. She at once said to me: "Mariana, here is the first copy of my book, and I give it to you." Taking a pencil she wrote on the fly-leaf, "With compliments of the author," and then handed it to me. I have the same book now.

I have also the first copy of the book containing the Spanish translation of "Ramona," which was sent me by the translator.

Naturally I am proud of the fact that Mrs. Jackson wished to make our home the home of Ramona; but greater honor have I always had, and greater comfort will I ever enjoy, in the fact that the gifted author, beloved of two continents, enshrined in the hearts of the people of the whole world, regarded me as her best friend.

Her name and her work are immortalized. Nothing I can say will add to her fame.

Mariana W. de Coronel

Los Angeles, July, 1913.

CHAPTER XVI

THE HOME OF RAMONA

WILLIAM A. ALDERSON

IT was Camulos ranch to which Helen Hunt Jackson was directed by Don Antonio de Coronel and his cultured wife.

To this ranch Mrs. Jackson journeyed. It was the estate of Don Ygnacio del Valle, and his widow, Doña Ysabel del Valle, was its owner and mistress.

Señora del Valle gave much of her life to humanitarian work, and being absent upon an errand of mercy upon the occasion of Mrs. Jackson's visit, did not see her; but her religious ardor and fidelity, so correctly portrayed in the character of Señora Moreno, was subsequently related to the author of "Ramona" by the Coronels.

That Camulos ranch was selected and intended as the home of Ramona is not to be questioned. Mrs. Jackson herself so declared, especially to the Coronels and to one of the authors of this volume, and the description in the story of the ranch and its appurtenances and surroundings positively identify it.

Mrs. Jackson was not disappointed. Chapter II of "Ramona" opens with this general statement of the ranch: "The Señora Moreno's house was one of the best specimens to be found in California of the representative house of the half-barbaric, half-elegant, wholly-generous and free-handed life led there by Mexican men and women of degree in the early part of this century, under the rule of the Spanish and Mexican viceroys. . . . It was a picturesque life, with more of sentiment and gaiety in it; more also that was truly dramatic; more romance than will ever be seen again on those sunny shores. The aroma of it all lingers there still; industries and inventions have not yet slain it; it will last out its century."

A visit to Camulos ranch on July 2, 1913, enables me to revoice the declaration that "the aroma of it all lingers there still." "The Señora Moreno's house" is there just as Mrs. Jackson saw and described it. There are the same white walls, the wide court verandas, "and a still broader one across the entire front, which looked to the south." There is the dining-room, "on the opposite side of the courtyard from the kitchen," and the same stairs leading from a higher to a lower part of the

THE WILLOWS AND SOUTH VERANDA, CAMULOS

(1) Under these trees were the washing stones where Alessandro first saw Ramona. (2) South veranda of Camulos dwelling, as it appeared in 1913.

(1) THE CROSS ON THE NORTH HILL, CAMULOS, OVERLOOKING THE RANCH

"She caused to be set up upon every one of the soft rounded hills * * * a large wooden cross, * * * that the heretics may know, when they go by, that they are on the estate of a good Catholic." "*Ramona.*" (2) To the left the plank fence on which Margarita hung the altar cloth, and from which it was blown and then torn, the bells, cross and famous little chapel, Camulos, as they appeared 1913.

south veranda, where Alessandro sat and played his violin to the stricken Felipe. Father Salvierderra's room, at the southeast corner of the house, and the barred window through which Ramona "saw Alessandro pacing up and down the walk" in the moonlight and by which she sat, peering sadly and wistfully into the night, made a prisoner by the angered Señora Moreno when discovered by her in the arms of Alessandro in the willows—these are there, just as Mrs. Jackson saw and described them.

On the hills to the north and south are the identical crosses described in the story of "Ramona," erected by Señora Moreno "that the heretics may know, when they go by, that they are on the estate of a good Catholic, and that the faithful may be reminded to pray." There they still stand, "summer and winter, rain and shine, the silent, solemn, outstretched arms"—the Blessed Cross, the sudden sight of which has wrought miracles of conversion on the most hardened. "Certain it is that many a good Catholic halted and crossed himself when he first beheld them in the lonely places, standing out in sudden relief against the blue sky."

The identical little chapel, "dearer to the Señora than her house," with its white sides, in a setting of orange trees, is still there. Its altar is yet "surrounded by a really imposing row of holy and apostolic figures." Its chests yet contain the most costly and elaborate vestments, some so heavily braided with gold as almost to be able to stand alone.

This chapel is a part of the history of the Catholic Church in California. Services are held within its historic and sacred portals as of old. Priests, many of them high dignitaries of the Church, visit it, that they may be able to say they officiated at its altar. Some bring their own vestments, not knowing what the chests of the chapel contain, and are astonished when shown the beautiful, gold-braided robes long kept and used in this miniature house of worship. Certain religious privileges have been granted to this little chapel which give to it a special character.

The chapel is only a frail frame building, the interior being twenty feet long and fourteen feet wide. Connected with the front is a roofed arcade, sides open and floored, thirty feet long and fourteen feet wide. In this arched addition are long benches running along the sides, for those who cannot find room within.

The torn altar cloth is still in existence and use, though not the only one that adorns the altar from time to time. This particular piece was made from Señora del Valle's wedding gown. It is the subject of one of the most interesting and eventful climaxes of the story. The fence on which Margarita hung this altar adornment to dry after washing it, preparatory to the coming of Father Salvierderra, is still intact. It divides the yard from the artichoke patch, into which the cloth was blown and then dragged and torn by Capitan, Juan Canito's favorite collie.

There is the same wide, straight walk, shaded by a trellis, that leads down to the brook and the willow trees, where were "the broad flat stone washboards, on which was done all the family washing." But the brook is now to the north, nearer the house. The trellis is not now "so knotted and twisted with grapevines that little" of the woodwork is to be seen, but grapevines are vigorously climbing over it.

The big gnarled willow tree, under which were the flat stone washboards, and in the evening shadows of which Alessandro first beheld Ramona, is still at the foot of the arbor. The pomegranate trees yet mark the border of the orange grove in front of the house.

"The little graveyard on the hillside," where the Señora Moreno was "laid by the side of her husband and her children," with its picket fence and wooden crosses, still bears its awful silence in the shadow of a single pepper tree.

The gray stone bowls, "hollowed and polished, shining inside and out," "made by the Indians, nobody knew how many ages ago, . . . with only stones for tools," which were used as flower pots, now adorn the rim of the cement fountain which is in the orange trees near the chapel.

Four shepherd dogs, the common ranch breed, answered the call for dinner, and suggested their illustrious forefather Capitan, Juan Canito's favorite collie, which went away in the stillness of that tragic night with Ramona and Alessandro, when they eloped from Camulos ranch and fled to Temecula. "The dogs, the poultry, all loved the sight of Ramona."

And there is yet to be seen the same public road which the commissioners located in the rear of the house, concerning which Señora Moreno exclaimed: "It is well. Let their travel be where it belongs, behind our kitchen, and no one have sight of the front doors of our houses, except friends who have come to visit us. . . . Whenever she saw passing the place wagons or carriages belonging to the hated Americans, it gave her a distinct thrill

GRAPE ARBOR AND OLIVE MILL

(1) The grape arbor, Camulos, leading to the washing stones, as it appeared 1913. (2) The olive mill and tank, Camulos, 1913.

INNER COURT AND OLD WINERY, CAMULOS

(1) Inner court, Camulos, as it appeared 1913. (2) The old winery, Camulos, as it appeared 1913. "Every hand on the place was hard at work, picking the grapes, treading them out in tubs, and emptying the juice into stretched rawhides swung from crossbeams." *"Ramona"*

of pleasure to think that the house turned its back on them." This road is now the main county thoroughfare through the Santa Clara Valley, in which is located Camulos ranch.

The winery, where the finest of vintages were pressed and the juice aged to a perfect nectar, still stands, though now but a storehouse for abandoned casks and ranch implements. And there, under a cottonwood tree, is the same *mortero* used in making olive oil in the days long gone by.

Less than a hundred feet from the chapel, and in line with the picket fence in its rear, is an oak frame from which, at the time of Mrs. Jackson's visit, hung three Mission bells. They were brought from Spain, and had done long service in one of the old Franciscan Missions in California. These bells were swung in the shape of a triangle. The top one was used to call to meals, the largest to summon those on the ranch to chapel, and the third to call the children to school. The belfry frame, with two of the bells, remains undisturbed, evidencing the old days on this splendid hacienda. The missing bell was taken away some time ago by one of the daughters of Señora del Valle, Mrs. Josefa Forster, and placed in the chapel erected at her residence in Los Angeles, where it does appropriate service to this day.

There is also still standing the large white cross just within the picket fence near the chapel.

Although not of sufficient size at the time of Mrs. Jackson's visit to attract attention, there is now, to the west of the house about one hundred feet, the largest English walnut tree known. Its trunk measures six feet in diameter, and its branches extend fifty-two feet from the body of the tree in every direction. Beneath its ample shade are a number of chairs cut from the trunks of big orange trees, in which one may comfortably recline on the hottest day.

Only a few minor changes have taken place since Mrs. Jackson's visit. The chief industry is no longer the rearing of sheep. The sweeping acres are in a high state of cultivation. Fruit-pickers have superseded sheep-shearers. Semi-tropical fruits and grain constitute the principal crops.

The almond orchard has given way to oranges. The sheep-shearing sheds and corrals are no more. Large barns, stables and pens have supplanted the old corrals and tule-covered sheds.

"The second willow copse, which lay perhaps a quarter of a mile west of the first," where Ramona met Alessandro on his return from Temecula the night they stole away from the Señora Moreno's, is gone, washed away by a flood in the Santa Clara River; and the garden of flowers in front of the house is now a part of the orange grove "between the veranda and the river meadows."

Camulos ranch is still owned by the del Valle family. On the day of my visit there, July 2, 1913, I was cordially received by Don Ulpiano del Valle, one of the sons, who is in active charge of the ranch and resides there. Mr. Charles H. Cram and his wife, who was Miss Ysabel del Valle, a daughter of Doña Ysabel del Valle, were visiting the ranch on that day.

Though I have many times passed through Camulos on the train, I had never before stopped there. Mr. Cram spent the day with me, and was especially courteous and obviously pleased in pointing out many features described or named in "Ramona," explaining in detail the changes wrought.

Upon the occasion of his first visit to Camulos, Christmas time, twenty-five years previous, Mr. Cram said there were seventy-two guests present. Of the hospitality of the ranch Mrs. Jackson wrote: "Nobody ever knew exactly how many women were in the kitchen, or how many men in the fields. There were always women cousins, or brothers' wives or widows or daughters, who had come to stay, or men cousins, or sisters' husbands or sons, who were stopping on their way up or down the valley. When it came to the pay-roll, Señor Felipe knew to whom he paid wages; but who were fed and lodged under his roof, that was quite another thing. It could not enter into the head of a Mexican gentleman to make either count or account of that. It would be a disgraceful, niggardly thought. . . . In the General's day it had been a free-handed boast of his that never less than fifty persons, men, women and children, were fed within his gates each day; how many more, he did not care nor know. . . . Hardly a day passed that the Señora had not visitors. She was still a person of note; her house the natural resting place for all who journeyed through the valley."

I sat on the court veranda during the preparation of the noon meal, to which I was invited with cultured and gracious insistence. The feelings which obsessed me were indescribably intense. I knew the name and life of every character mentioned in the "Ramona" story, and they lived again in the dreamy fancy that possessed me. There were little ones, some the grandchildren of Señora del Valle, playing about the kitchen, replica of the scene witnessed by Mrs. Jackson and which inspired the sentence: "The troop of youngsters which still swarmed around the kitchen quarters of Señora Moreno's house, almost as numerous and inexplicable as in the grand old days of the General's time." I saw the servants carrying from the kitchen to the dining-room, "on the opposite side of the court-yard," dishes of steaming food; and on entering the dining-room the generous table recalled Mrs. Jackson's description of a meal at Camulos ranch: "A great dish of spiced beef and cabbage in the center of the table; a tureen of thick soup, with forcemeat balls and red peppers in it; two red earthen platters heaped, one with boiled rice and onions, the other with the delicious *frijoles* (beans) so dear to all Mexican hearts; cut-glass dishes filled with hot stewed pears, or preserved quinces, or grape jelly."

I stood on every spot of Camulos ranch mentioned in "Ramona." I climbed the hill to the north and reverently bowed before one of the Señora's crosses, and, though a "heretic," realized that I "was on the estate of a good Catholic." In fancy I saw Juan Canito, the head shepherd, again in life, on "the sunny veranda of the south side of the kitchen wing of the house," sitting "on the low bench, his head leaning back against the whitewashed wall, his long legs stretched out nearly across the whole width of the veranda, his pipe firmly wedged in the extreme left corner of his mouth, his hands in his pockets—the picture of placid content." Again there were the Indian sheep-shearers, "forms, dusky black against the fiery western sky, coming down the valley." Under the identical willow tree described in the story I could see Ramona, "her hair in disorder, her sleeves pinned loosely on her shoulders, her whole face aglow with the earnestness of her task," bending "low over the stones, rinsing the altar cloth up and down in the water, anxiously scanning it, then plunging it in again."

And how thrilling it was to complete the picture! "It was the band of Indian sheep-shearers. They turned to the left, and went toward the sheep sheds and booths. But there was one of them that Ramona did not see. He had been standing for some minutes concealed behind a large willow tree a few rods from the

WEST VERANDA AND BELLS, CAMULOS

West veranda, inner court, Camulos, as it appeared 1913.

Two of the three Mission bells at Camulos, 1913.

NORTH SIDE OF KITCHEN AND PUBLIC ROAD

(1) North side of kitchen and shepherd dogs, Camulos, 1913. "The dogs, the poultry, all loved the sight of Ramona." "*Ramona.*" (2) The public road behind Camulos dwelling, as it appeared 1913. "Whenever she saw passing the place wagons or carriages belonging to the hated Americans, it gave her a distinct thrill of pleasure to think that the house turned its back on them." "*Ramona.*"

place where Ramona was kneeling. It was Alessandro, son of Pablo Assis, captain of the sheep-shearing band. Walking slowly along in advance of his men, he had felt a light, as from a mirror held in the sun, smite his eyes. It was the red sunbeam on the glittering water where Ramona knelt. In the same second he saw Ramona. He halted, as wild creatures of the forest halt at a sound, gazed, walked abruptly away from his men, who kept on, not noticing his disappearance. Cautiously he moved a few steps nearer, into the shelter of the gnarled old willow, from behind which he could gaze unperceived on the beautiful vision —for so it seemed to him."

I could see Alessandro and Ramona in the darkness of the night in which they went out into a homeless world, with love as their only hope and courage, "under the willows—the same copse where he first halted at his first sight of Ramona"; could hear his soft Indian voice telling her he thought of her as "Majel," and saying to her, "it is the name of the bird you are like—the wood-dove—in the Luiseno tongue. . . . It is by that name I have often thought of you since the night I watched all night for you, after you kissed me, and two wood-doves were calling and answering each other in the dark; . . . and the wood-dove is true to its mate always."

There was Marda, the old cook, again officiating in the kitchen; Margarita, "the youngest and prettiest of the housemaids," agitated and sobbing because, through her negligence, the altar cloth had blown into the artichoke patch and been torn by Capitan, the shepherd dog; Juanita, the eldest of the house servants, silly, "good for nothing except to shell beans."

And there again was the Señora Moreno, "so quiet, so reserved, so gentle an exterior never was known to veil such an imperious and passionate nature, brimful of storm, always passing through stress; never thwarted, except at peril of those who did it; adored and hated by turn, and each at the hottest. A tremendous force wherever she appeared."

It was not difficult to picture the Señora bending over Felipe as he lay ill with fever in the raw-hide bed made by Alessandro, on the raised part of the south veranda, from which stairs lead to the lower portion. I sat on these steps, and fancied I could see Alessandro as he played his violin to soothe the suffering Felipe, his music at all times sad and plaintive because of his love for Ramona.

In the valley in which Camulos ranch is located I have seen the wild mustard growing just as described in "Ramona"—"in the branches of which the birds of the air may rest. . . . With a clear blue sky behind it . . . it looks like a golden snow storm." It is a beautiful picture drawn by Mrs. Jackson of the meeting of Father Salvierderra and Ramona in the mustard.

Father Salvierderra! His is the strong, towering, grand character of "Ramona"! I stood in the room in the southeast corner of the ranch dwelling always reserved for this saintly man. I felt I was on a hallowed spot. "It had a window to the south and one to the east. When the first glow of dawn came in the sky, this eastern window was lit up as by a fire. The Father was always on watch for it, having usually been at prayer for hours. As the first ray reached the window he would throw the casement wide open, and standing there with bared head, strike up the melody of the sunrise hymn sung in all devout Mexican families."

From this room I went to the little chapel, with its white walls, set in the orange grove. The night of the angered scene between Señora Moreno and Ramona, when the Señora discovered Ramona in Alessandro's arms at the willows which shade the washing stones at the brook, Alessandro "hid behind the geranium clump at the chapel door . . . watching Ramona's window, . . . racked by his emotions; . . . Ramona loved him; she had told him so."

Passing through the arched approach, the door of the chapel was opened. Silently I entered. A taper was burning. There was the altar, still "surrounded by a really imposing row of holy and apostolic figures." There was the same torn altar cloth, so deftly repaired by Ramona that the rent in it might not be noticed; but it did not escape the keen and observing eyes of Helen Hunt Jackson.

What thoughts seized me! How vividly real seemed all that is in the "Ramona" story concerning this sacred place! I could see "the chapel full of kneeling men and women; those who could not find room inside kneeling on the garden walks; Father Salvierderra, in gorgeous vestments, coming, at close of the services, slowly down the aisle, the close-packed rows of worshipers parting to right and left to let him through, all looking up eagerly for his blessing, women giving him offerings of fruit

INTERIOR OF CAMULOS CHAPEL

"In the little chapel in the garden the altar was surrounded by a really imposing row of holy and apostolic figures." *"Ramona."*

VERANDA OF INNER COURT AND WALNUT TREE

(1) Part of the veranda on inner court, Camulos, 1913. (2) Under the largest English walnut tree known, Camulos, 1913.

or flowers, and holding up their babies, that he might lay his hands on their heads."

Father Salvierderra! Consecrated to the tenets and purposes of the Catholic Church; trudging over mountain and through valley from his home, the Santa Barbara Mission, to cheer and bless the humble and the high alike. "To wear a shoe in place of a sandal, to take money in a purse for a journey, above all to lay aside the gray gown and cowl for any sort of secular garment, seemed to him wicked. To own comfortable clothes while there were others suffering for want of them—and there were always such—seemed to him a sin for which one might not undeservedly be smitten with sudden and terrible punishment. In vain the Brothers again and again supplied him with a warm cloak; he gave it away to the first beggar he met." "What can I do to help you?" was the ever-ready question that revealed his unselfish and sympathetic nature.

And there in this chapel, a holy spot in the wilderness, I stood with bowed head and solemn thought, touched by the memory and spirit of this grand, this noble Franciscan; "so revered and loved by all who had come under his influence, that they would wait long months without the offices of the church, rather than confess their sins or confide their perplexities to anyone else." I was impelled to cry out, as though in his living presence, as did Agrippa to Paul, "Almost thou persuadest me to be a Christian."

CHAPTER XVII

ABBOT KINNEY, CO-COMMISSIONER WITH MRS. JACKSON—N. H. MITCHELL

NOW known as "The Doge of Venice," his present abode, the beautiful and popular seaside resort near Los Angeles which he founded, Mr. Abbot Kinney is enjoying the fruits of a long and successful life.

He came to California in 1873, and was a guest at the famous old Kimball Mansion on New High Street, Los Angeles, when Mrs. Jackson stopped there on her first visit to the State.

The vivacity, wit, culture and genius of the woman attracted Mr. Kinney. He was a friend to the Mission Indians, was in deep sympathy with the purpose of Mrs. Jackson's trip to California, and soon a close friendship was created between them, which resulted in Mr. Kinney being selected by Mrs. Jackson as co-commissioner to aid in her struggling effort to protect the various Indian tribes in Southern California.

Mrs. Jackson's selection of Mr. Kinney to accompany and aid her was little less than an inspiration. He was familiar with the ground to be covered, had some knowledge of the subject to be considered, and was not wholly a stranger to the Spanish language or the mixed dialects of the various tribes of Indians whose villages were to be visited. Moreover, he had come to share in the earnestness and enthusiasm with which the noble woman entered upon her mission. He recognized her as the leading spirit in the humanitarian movement, and addressed her as "General." She, in turn, regarded him as her "Comrade," and so addressed him, later, in her correspondence, shortening the appellation to "Co."

In their wanderings over the San Jacinto Mountains it became necessary to visit localities that could not be reached in any sort of vehicle. Mr. Kinney naturally relieved Mrs. Jackson in so far as he could from these arduous tasks. In doing so he met with some incidents not witnessed by his chief. Some of these were related by Mr. Kinney to the authors of this volume. One instance is of peculiar human interest. A man named Fayne had wrongfully dispossessed an Indian of his home, and was holding possession when Mr. Kinney was in the neighborhood. It was a singularly aggravating outrage, and Commissioner Kin-

MR. ABBOT KINNEY,

Co-commissioner and intimate friend of Helen Hunt Jackson, who journeyed with her through Southern California, and aided in her work for the Mission Indians.

SAN GABRIEL MISSION

As it appeared at the time Mrs. Jackson saw it. One of the missing bells is at the late E. J Baldwin's Santa Anita ranch. The other was given to and is now at the Church of the Angels, Los Angeles.

ney determined to dispossess him while on the ground, if possible, and to that extent right the wrong.

As he approached the house on horseback he observed a man leaning over the front gate with a rifle in his hand and a set look of wicked determination in his eyes. Mr. Kinney affected not to observe the bellicose attitude of the villain, and although the weapon was pointed at him, rode directly up to the fence.

"Well," said Fayne, in a brutal tone of voice, "what do you want here?"

"I am an agent of the Government," answered Mr. Kinney, "and I've come to investigate your title to this property. I've heard the Indian's story, and now I've come to hear what you have to say."

"Oh, well, that's different. If you want to be decent about the matter and do the right thing, I don't mind telling you what my claim is."

With this Fayne lowered his rifle and invited Mr. Kinney into the house. His story was long and rambling, but wholly without merit, and Mr. Kinney and Mrs. Jackson, before leaving the locality, had the satisfaction of restoring the little ranch to its rightful owner, the Indian who had lived on it all his life, as had his father before him.

Upon another occasion it became necessary for Mr. Kinney to go on foot to a little ranch on the edge of the desert, where he found the owner, an aged Indian, in great distress over the complete destruction of his crop—sole reliance for the sustenance of himself and family until another could be grown—by a white man named Lugo, who had driven a herd of cattle and a band of sheep over it, breaking down the fences on either side, and leaving not a vestige of vegetation upon the place. The act was one of pure malevolence, since there was an abundance of room on either side of the ranch to have driven his stock without damage to anyone.

Mr. Kinney burned with indignation when he viewed the wreck and heard the pitiful story from the lips of the sufferer. Seeking out the perpetrator he introduced himself as an agent of the Government, told him he had appraised the damage, and warned him that, unless he should appear at a certain place in San Diego within ten days and deposit the sum named for the benefit of the outraged Indian, he would send an officer after him. There was no parleying, nor was there any subsequent default. Mr. Kinney and Mrs. Jackson were able to hand the money over to the grateful Indian a few weeks later.

Particularly interesting was Mr. Kinney's relation of the visit of Mrs. Jackson to Temecula. He was with her on that momentous occasion. The scenes of desolation, mute but irrefutable evidence of the outrage of the whites upon the Indians, seemed to wrack the heart and mind of Mrs. Jackson. The interview between her and Mrs. Wolfe, Mrs. Hartsel of "Ramona," was fervent and dramatic. Mrs. Wolfe had witnessed the ejectment of the Indians from Temecula. Her sympathies were with the maltreated red men, and naturally she elicited the confidence and admiration of Mrs. Jackson.

At the Temecula graveyard Mrs. Jackson observed an Indian woman weeping over the grave of her husband. The incident gave birth to the character of Carmena in "Ramona." "As they entered the enclosure a dark figure arose from one of the graves. . . . It was Carmena. The poor creature, nearly crazed with grief, was spending her days by her baby's grave in Pachanga, and her nights by her husband's in Temecula. She dared not come to

Temecula by day, for the Americans were there, and she feared them."

When in a reminiscent mood Mr. Kinney relates many interesting incidents associated with the historical journey over the San Jacinto Mountains, originally suggested to Mrs. Jackson by the Coronels, and which gave birth to the great American romance, "Ramona." He asserts that nearly if not quite all of the characters and incidents in "Ramona" were suggested by persons seen and episodes encountered during the journey and Mrs. Jackson's visit to Camulos ranch, and that the author's description of places, relation of incidents and portrayal of characters are astonishingly correct and faithful.

While Mr. Kinney, with his accustomed courtesy, talked willingly and at length with the authors concerning Mrs. Jackson and "Ramona," to the request that he contribute something to this volume over his own signature he answered: "I could not write anything on the subject that would not be either dull or colorless, or violate my views on the sacred character of the relations of personal friendship."

The close and intimate friendship existing between Mrs. Jackson and Mr. Kinney is evi-

INTERIOR OF SAN GABRIEL MISSION

SAN DIEGO MISSION

"Here was the spot where that grand old Franciscan, Padre Junipero Serra, began his work * * * to reclaim the wilderness. * * * Here he baptized his first Indian converts, and founded his first mission. And the only traces now remaining of his heroic labors * * * were a pile of crumbling [illegible]"

denced by the correspondence between them. Portions of some of the letters of the author of "Ramona" to Mr. Kinney are here given:

New York, January 17, 1884.

Dear Co.:

. . . .

When I arrived here on Nov. 20 and found that you had left on November 19, "a madder man than Mr. Mears you would not wish to see."—You surely could not have got my note saying I would start on the 16th—I took cold on the journey. . . .

Feby. 2. Whether from the horrible weather or from overwork I don't know, I collapsed for a week, and had an ugly sore throat and did no work. Now I am all right again and back at my table, but shall go slower. I am leading a life as quiet as if I were at Mrs. Kimball's—I go nowhere—am never out after 5 P.M. I am resolved to run no risks whatever till after I get this story done. I hope it is good. It is over one-third done. Am pretty sure the 1st of March will see it done. Then I will play.

The weather has been horrible—snow after snow; raw and cloudy days,—I have sighed for Southern California.

But in the house I have been comfortable—have not once seen the mercury below 60 in my rooms. The apartment is sunny and light—6th floor—east windows—all my "traps," as Mr. Jackson calls them, came in well, and the room looks as if I had lived in it all my life.

Now, for yourself—What have you done? How are you running your home?—Who is at the Villa? Is Mrs. Carr well? My regards to her. Don't you wish you had carried home a wife? I am exceedingly disappointed that you didn't.

Miss Sheriff writes me that a suit is brought for the ejectment of the Saboba Indians. Let me know if you have heard of it—what Brunson & Wells say. I wrote to Wells a long time ago asking for information about the suit by which the Temecula Indians were ejected—but he has not replied.

What do you hear of the new agent?

I got Miss Sheriff's salary restored to old figure.

I have just sent a list of 200 names to Com. Price to mail our report to. Of course you had copies. I feel well satisfied with it. Do not you? I wish they'd send us again somewhere. They never will. I've had my last trip as a "Junketing Female Commissioner."

Do write soon;—and answer all my questions—and don't wait for me to reply, but write again. I am writing from 1,000 to 2,000 words a day on the story and letters are impossible, except to Mr. Jackson. Whether I write or not you know I am always the same affectionate old General.

Yours ever,

H. J.

The "story" to which reference is made was "Ramona," which was being written at the date of the letter.

New York, February 20th, 1884.

Dear Co.:

Your first letter made me wretched. If we had "been and gone" and got a rascally firm set over those Indian matters I thought we might better never have been born.

But your second reassures me.

I sent you one of the reports. You can get all you want, I think, by writing to Commissioner Price. I sent him a long list of names to mail it to. They said I could have all I wanted. Of course you can too. There is a bill of some sort, prepared and before Congress. I have written to Teller asking for it, or sum and substance. He does not reply. None of them care for anything now, except the election. . . .

I am working away at the story (Ramona)—twenty chapters done. I'd like to consult you. Do you think it will do any harm to depart from the chronological sequence of events in my story?

For dramatic purposes I have put the Temecula ejectment before the first troubles in San Pasquale.

Will anybody be idiot enough to make a point of that? I am not writing history. I hope the story is good.

I wish you could see my rooms. What with Indian baskets, the things from Marsh's, and antique rugs, they are really quite charming, luckily for me who have been shut up in them by the solid week.

Such weather was never seen. There are no words—proper ones—suitable to describe it. I sigh for San Gabriel sunshine.

I hope you are well and jolly. I'm awfully sorry you are not married. Good night. Always, Affectionately yours,

General.

Regards to Mrs. Crank, Mrs. C——, etc. I don't wonder the latter does not succeed as landlady. I'd as soon board with a cyclone.

PAGE OF OLD RECORD AND BELL, SAN GABRIEL

(1) Page of old record at San Gabriel Mission, written by Father Junipero Serra and containing his signature. (2) One of the missing bells from San Gabriel Mission, taken by the late E. J. ("Lucky") Baldwin, as hung on his Santa Anita ranch.

INDIAN MISSION SCHOOL, SAN DIEGO

The following letter was written after the completion of "Ramona," and Mrs. Jackson had fallen down the stairs in her home at Colorado Springs and fractured her leg.

Colorado Springs,
September 28th, 1884.

Dear Co.:

. . . .

I am thinking of coming to So. California as soon as I can hobble. I must fly from here before November, but I do not feel quite up to shutting myself in for the winter as I must in New York. So I propose to run across to your snug seashore—for two or three months of sunshine and outdoors—before going to New York. Do you not think that wise?

I wrote to Mrs. W—— in San Diego—the only place I know in all California where there was real comfort. Also I like the San Diego climate best. But I learned to my great disappointment that she had gone to Los Angeles. The N's urge my coming to a new hotel in San Diego—but I have a mortal dread of California hotels. Do you know anything of it?—And do you know where Mrs. W's house in Los Angeles is? If it is on high ground? . . .

. . . I shall bring my Effie with me—too

helpless yet to travel alone. Goodness! What martyrdom crutches are! While I was stationary in bed it was fun in comparison with this. But I am a sinner to grumble. I shall walk with one crutch and one cane, next week, the doctor thinks, and that is great luck for such a bad compound fracture as mine; and at my age. My weight also is a sad hindrance. If I weighed only 125 or so they say I could walk with a cane now. Ultimately—they insist—my leg will be as good as ever, and no lameness. I shall believe it when I see it! . . .

I had a letter from Mrs. C—— the other day. Strange, that disorderly chaotic woman writes a precise, methodical hand, clear as type, characterless in its precision; and I, who am a martinet of ardent system, write—well—as you see! What nonsense to say handwriting shows character.

I have ordered a copy of "The Hunter Cats of Connorloa" sent to you. You will laugh to see yourself saddled with an orphan niece and nephew. I hope you won't dislike the story. I propose in the next to make you travel all through Southern California with "Susy and Rea"—and tell the Indian story over again. I only hope that scalawag C——, of Los Angeles, will come across the story, and see himself set forth in it. He will recognize the story of Fernando, the old Indian he turned out at San Gabriel.

As you recollect the situation of lands at Saboba was there good land enough in that neighborhood for those Indians to get homes? The Indian appropriation bill passed in July has a clause enabling Indians to take land under homestead laws, with no fees.

What are Brunson and Wells doing? Anything? What is the state of the Saboba matter? But I suppose you can think of nothing save politics till next Dec.

Write soon. I want to know about Mrs. W's house—if it is high, sunny, airy, etc.

Yours always,

General.

Having passed several months in Los Angeles, Mrs. Jackson went to San Francisco early in 1885, where she died a few months later.

San Francisco, April 1st, 1885.

Dear Co.:

I don't wonder you thought so. Anybody well enough to journey to S. F. wouldn't seem to be in such bad case. But it was true—I came up here on my last shred of nerve force, and collapsed at once. I have had a terrible poisoning. It will be seven weeks next Saturday since there has been any proper action of either stomach or bowels,—simply six weeks of starvation, that is all, and the flesh has rained off me. I must have lost at least forty pounds, and I am wan and yellow in the face. Nothing ever before so utterly upset me. Everybody cried that bade me good-by, I looked so ill. Even Miller, my driver, stood speechless, before me in the cars—with his eyes full of tears! Dear old Mr. Coronel put his arms round me sighing: "Excuse me, I must!" Embraced me in Spanish fashion with a half sob. I know they none of them expected me to live—which did not cheer me up much. I seemed to be better at first after getting here, but had a relapse last week—diarrhœa as bad as ever and stomach worse. I am in bed—take only heated milk and gr—and sit up long enough to have my bed made. It is a bad job, old fellow, and I doubt very much if I ever pull out of it. It's all right, only if I had been asked to choose the one city of all I know in which I would have most disliked to be slain, it would have been San Francisco.

Thursday, A.M. Your note is just here.

Sorry you have to change cooks. Changing stomachs is worse, however. Don't grumble, lest a worse thing befall you. Give as much of my love as your wife will accept, to her. I liked your calling her the "Young H. H." There is no doubt she looks as I did at twenty. . . . I shall never be well again, Co. I know it with a certain knowledge. Nobody at my age with my organization ever really got over a severe blood poisoning. My doctor is a good one, a young man—Dr. Boericke, 834 Sutter St. I like him heartily. He is clever, enthusiastic, European taught. All that homeopathy can do for me I shall have, and you know the absoluteness of my faith in homeopathy. Good-by. I'll let you know how it goes. Don't give yourself a moment's worry.

Yours always,

General.

P. S. Can't you do something to get Rust appointed Indian agent? I have heard quite directly that Lamar is full of warm sympathy for the Indians. Do try, Co., and accomplish something for them. You might, if you would determine to.

Although approaching the sere and yellow-leaf period of his useful sojourn here below,

Mr. Kinney is still a very active man, daily to be seen at his desk in "Venice of America."

The carriage in which Mrs. Jackson commenced her journey through Southern California was owned and driven by Mr. N. H. Mitchell, who now resides in Los Angeles. The start was made from Anaheim, twenty-six miles from Los Angeles. The occupants of the carriage were Mrs. Jackson, Mr. Abbot Kinney, Mr. Henry Sandham and Mr. N. H. Mitchell. Mr. Mitchell has contributed this statement of his association with Mrs. Jackson:

"I first met Mrs. Helen Hunt Jackson at Anaheim, near Los Angeles, in April, 1883. She came there in company with Mr. Abbot Kinney and Mr. Henry Sandham, the artist.

"Mrs. Jackson was seeking someone who was familiar with the country and could guide her and her companions through Southern California, and especially to the several Indian settlements.

"I understood that she was in California as a representative of the U. S. Interior Department, especially authorized to visit the Mission Indians and report upon their condition,

MR. N H. MITCHELL,

Owner and driver of the carriage in which Helen Hunt Jackson made the first part of her journey through Southern California.

SAN JUAN CAPISTRANO MISSION

and recommend action to be taken by the Government in their behalf. She seemed intensely interested in the Indians at Temecula and Warner's Ranch.

"Our first stop was at San Juan Capistrano, where we remained two days. From there we visited the Santa Margarita Rancho, where we were guests at the palatial home of Don Juan Forster for two days.

"Our journey from place to place was attended by many exciting and interesting incidents. Mrs. Jackson accepted every inconvenience and hardship without complaint. She seemed wholly absorbed by the Indian subject: to hear, to see all concerning them. No detail escaped her. She was ever smiling, good-natured and witty, but always earnest and determined.

"We encountered many trying conditions, especially for a woman, and one of Mrs. Jackson's refinement. We often camped at night. Pala Mission, on the San Luis Rey River, was reached late at night, and there we were forced to camp. We found an American there, who was trading with the Indians, and prevailed upon him to give us some supper. Something about him particularly amused and interested Mr. Sandham, who named the fellow 'Garibaldi.' No beds could be had, and we had to sleep in a haystack.

"Mrs. Jackson made friends with all whom she met, both white people and Indians. She was attentive, kind and courteous to everyone.

"I kept the carriage in which we rode until a few years ago. I offered to give it to the Los Angeles Chamber of Commerce, that it might be preserved in connection with the Coronel Collection, but the offer was refused on the ground of lack of space. I finally sold it to a carriage dealer in Pasadena, who dissembled it and used its parts for various purposes.

"I know of many of the incidents of our travel to be the same as related in 'Ramona.' Mrs. Hartsel, whom Mrs. Jackson met at Temecula, was Mrs. Ramona Wolfe, the wife of the storekeeper there. Mrs. Jackson was greatly interested in Mrs. Wolfe, and from her learned many things concerning the Temecula Indians and their ejectment from their lands. Mrs. Wolfe was in sympathy with the Indians, and, therefore, Mrs. Jackson gave her special attention.

"Because Mrs. Wolfe's name was Ramona, and Mrs. Jackson seemed so particularly impressed by her, I have always thought she was the original of Mrs. Jackson's heroine in 'Ramona.' Mrs. Wolfe never lived at Camulos ranch, and never had, so far as I know, any of the experiences related in the novel as having attended Ramona."

CHAPTER XVIII

HENRY SANDHAM, THE ARTIST OF "RAMONA"

THE constant companion of Helen Hunt Jackson when in California on her Indian mission was the late Mr. Henry Sandham. He was one of the artists of the "Century Magazine," had established a reputation in his work and was selected and sent by the Century Company with Mrs. Jackson on her California journey.

Mrs. Jackson was to contribute articles to the magazine named, and Mr. Sandham to illustrate them, not with camera, but with pencil and brush.

Henry Sandham was born at Montreal, Canada, in 1842. It has been said that northern climes are too cold to nourish artistic temperament and talent; but out of the Canadian wintry blasts came Mr. Sandham, destined to rise to success and fame in the world of art.

The wild life of Canada was his special work, and his introduction in the United States was through the "Century Magazine," in which were published his sketches depicting the outdoor life of his native land.

MR. HENRY SANDHAM, ARTIST OF THE "CENTURY MAGAZINE,"

Who accompanied Mrs. Jackson to and on her journeys in California, and who illustrated her writings and painted the "Ramona" pictures. As he appeared in 1883, while in California.

SAN LUIS REY MISSION

" Alessandro * * * says, 'Look at San Luis Rey. Nothing but the garden and orchard left.' "
" Ramona."

Mr. Sandham has declared that, when a youth, every available minute, night and day, he pursued diligently and earnestly drawing, sketching and painting. Even the opposition of his parents to an artistic career did not discourage him.

In 1880 he was selected as one of the original members of the Royal Canadian Academy, which was founded by H. R. H., the Princess Louise. He then went to Europe, where, with the money he had made and saved, he pursued his studies. He soon returned to America and located at Boston, and it was while he was residing there that he was commissioned by the "Century Magazine" to accompany Mrs. Jackson to California. In later years he went to London, where he continued his work, and where he died, June 21, 1910.

The Century Company is entitled to the credit for the coming of Mrs. Jackson to California; she was its paid contributor. The Mission Indians were to be her principal theme; but the Franciscan Missions and Southern California were within the sphere of her commission.

The wisdom and business sagacity of the Century Company in securing the services of Mrs. Jackson for the work resulted in enriching the columns of its magazine with articles from Mrs. Jackson's pen, the best known and most generally read being, "Father Junipero and His Work," "The Present Condition of the Mission Indians in Southern California," and "Echoes in the City of Angels." These beautiful and historical compositions have been republished in two different forms: "Glimpses of Three Coasts," and "Glimpses of California and the Missions." The first two, "Father Junipero and His Work," and "The Present Condition of the Mission Indians in Southern California," are a part of the reading series in the public schools of California; credit for which is to be given to the thoughtfulness and persistency of Miss Annie B. Picher, of Pasadena, California, who has done much to popularize the works of Mrs. Jackson and honor her memory.

Mrs. Jackson's magazine contributions were elaborately and realistically illustrated by Mr. Sandham. He went everywhere with his principal. He visited every Mission, studied Indian character, and sketched from life. He himself has said that his sketches "were always made on the spot, with Mrs. Jackson close at hand suggesting emphasis to this object or prominence to that." This statement includes the drawings which embellish the "Pasadena Edition" of "Ramona"; was indeed uttered in direct reference to the novel.

"Glimpses of Three Coasts" and "Glimpses of California and the Missions" are valuable and worthy of space in every library because of the illustrations they contain alone.

It was not until 1900 that Mr. Sandham gave to the public the "Ramona" paintings from which were taken the illustrations contained in the "Pasadena Edition." This was seventeen years after making the sketches for them in California.

The illustrations proper number fifteen, every one being especially pertinent to the text. They make real and living things of their subjects. In addition there are twenty-six decorative chapter headings; all the work of Mr. Sandham.

This work alone places Mr. Sandham in the front rank of the world's artists. All are most beautiful and interesting, but to the authors the most appealing of these paintings is the one of the meeting of Ramona and Father Salvierderra in the wild mustard. The Father was expected at Camulos ranch on his annual pilgrimage, and Ramona went forth to greet him. The text thus pictures the scene: "The wild mustard in Southern California is like that spoken of in the New Testament, in the branches of which the birds of the air may rest. . . . The cloud of blossom seems floating in the air; at times it looks like golden dust. With a clear blue sky behind it, as it is often seen, it looks like a golden snow-storm. . . . Father Salvierderra soon found himself in a veritable thicket. . . . Suddenly he heard faint notes of singing. He paused,—listened. It was the voice of a woman. . . . The notes grew clearer, though still low and sweet as the twilight notes of the thrush. . . . Father Salvierderra stood still as one in a dream. . . . In a moment more came, distinct and clear to his ear, the beautiful words of the second stanza of Saint Francis' inimitable lyric, 'The Canticle of the Sun.' . . . 'Ramona!' exclaimed the Father. . . . And as he spoke her face came into sight, set in a swaying frame of the blossoms."

What more inspiring subject could there be to the artist? Mr. Sandham's genius poured into the picture he created, and the scene lives.

No less dramatic, however, are the other paintings, each a pictured climax in the sorrowful and stirring story of "Ramona." Every detail of fact was carefully and correctly sketched and colored by the artist. In the picture of the Señora Moreno reprimanding Juan Canito, the head shepherd, for denouncing Luigo, the lazy shepherd boy, the veranda on the west side of the court at Camulos ranch is readily recognized—even as it is at this time. The Señora had said to Juan, "I fear the Father will give you penance when he hears what you have said," and then turned her back, while he "stood watching her as she walked away, at her usual slow pace, her head slightly bent forward, her rosary lifted in her left hand, and the fingers of the right hand mechanically slipping the beads." The painting is in every detail true to the text.

The portraits of Ramona and Alessandro are idealized ones. In their faces are plainly depicted the intensity of their natures, their strong characters, their sufferings and their sorrows. These pictures are so strikingly true to the descriptions of the heroine and hero in the story as to be readily recognized. They reveal an undercurrent of woe that is the pathos of the romance.

Another of the paintings is a portrait of Father Salvierderra, in cowl and cassock, a cross with the Savior pendent from the neck. It was, as before stated, seventeen years after

Mr. Sandham had seen the original of Father Salvierderra at Santa Barbara Mission, Father Francisco de Jesus Sanchez, O.F.M., that he produced the painting of Father Salvierderra for "Ramona." It would seem that the artist desired to idealize the priestly character. The face is uplifted, the eyes turned toward heaven. All eyes are beautiful when looking heavenward. In the portrait are strongly portrayed those intensely devout, unselfish and saintly virtues attributed to Father Salvierderra in the romance, and actually possessed by his prototype, Father Sanchez.

In the description of Father Salvierderra, when journeying from Santa Barbara Mission to Camulos ranch, pausing many times to gaze at the beautiful flowers that lined his pathway, Mr. Sandham found inspiration for the painting of the Father standing, leaning on his staff, viewing the scene about him. "Flowers were always dear to the Franciscans," is the quotation from the story that designates this painting. This picture brings realization to this text of the story: "It was melancholy to see how, after each one of these pauses, each fresh drinking in of the beauty of the landscape and the balmy air, the old man resumed his slow pace, with a long sigh and

THE ALTAR IN THE CHAPEL AT CAMULOS

The rent in the altar cloth repaired by Ramona, on the right.

CHURCH OF THE ANGELS, AT THE PLAZA, LOS ANGELES,

Connected with which was the Convent of the Sacred Heart. "She (Ramona) had had two years at school in the Convent of the Sacred Heart, Los Angeles. * * * Here she had won the affection of all the Sisters, who spoke of her habitually as the 'blessed child.'" "*Ramona*."

his eyes cast down. The fairer this beautiful land, the sadder to know it lost to the Church —alien hands reaping its fullness, establishing new customs, new laws. All the way down the coast from Santa Barbara he had seen, at every stopping place, new tokens of the settling up of the country—farms opening, towns growing; the Americans pouring in at all points to reap the advantage of their new possession. It was this which had made his journey heavy-hearted, and made him feel, in approaching the Señora Moreno's, as if he were coming to one of the last sure strongholds of the Catholic faith left in the country."

When Felipe, not yet recovered from a recent fever, undertook to assist at the sheep-shearing, he fainted on the top of the shed where he was at work packing the wool. There was confusion and anxiety because of the difficulty incident to removing him to the ground. It was Alessandro who sprang up the cleated post, seized Felipe and carried him along a plank to a place of safety. It was a tragic moment, and the scene is vividly delineated by Mr. Sandham in another of the paintings.

During Felipe's illness nearly every day Alessandro was sent for to play his violin or sing to him. One of the paintings is of Felipe's bedroom, the Señora Moreno sitting by her stricken son, and Alessandro, with violin and bow at ease, singing. "It seemed to be the only thing that roused him from his half lethargic state." Felipe would say to Alessandro, "I am going to sleep now, sing." The artist impressively presents the sick-room scene, the anxious watching of the devoted mother, the ardor and seriousness of the Indian singer.

A thrilling scene is presented by the painting portraying Señora Moreno enraged at the discovery of Ramona locked in the arms of Alessandro under the willows at the washing stones in the twilight. With the stamping of her foot, and directing with outstretched arm, she ordered Alessandro out of her sight; but "Alessandro did not stir, except to turn toward Ramona with an inquiring look." Señora Moreno is pictured in extreme coldness, hatred and anger, Alessandro in despair, Ramona in dignified protest; the whole eliciting sympathy for the lovers, disdain for the Señora.

A pathetic part of the "Ramona" story is the journeying of Alessandro and the heroine on horseback from Camulos ranch to Temecula and thence on to their place of marriage, San Diego. "Baba and Benito," the respective

MR. HENRY SANDHAM AS HE APPEARED A YEAR BEFORE HIS DEATH

GREVEJA PA AND MISSION INDIANS

(1) Greveja Pa, the oldest woman of the Temecula Indians. (2) A band of Mission Indian shearers. "It was sheep-shearing time in Southern California. * * * Forms, dusky black against the fiery sky, were coming down the valley It was the band of Indian shearers." "*Ramona.*"

names of Ramona's horse and Alessandro's, "were now such friends they liked to pace closely side by side; and Baba and Benito were by no means without instinctive recognitions of the sympathy between their riders . . . Baba had long ago learned to stop when his mistress laid her hand on Alessandro's shoulder. He stopped now, and it was long minutes before he had the signal to go on again." And here was a demonstration of the love that inflamed Alessandro and compelled him to despair because of his abject poverty in worldly goods, causing him to cry out to Ramona, "'Majella! Majella! . . . What can Alessandro do now? What, oh, what? Majella gives all; Alessandro gives nothing!'; and he bowed his forehead on her hands before he put them back gently on Baba's neck." Mr. Sandham's temperament was in accord with this touching episode, which is the subject of one of the most interesting of his "Ramona" paintings.

A demonstration of implicit trust of woman in man and of religious fidelity of the latter in reciprocation is the experience of Ramona and Alessandro in the mountains the first night after their elopement from Señora Moreno's. "Before nightfall of this, their first day in the wilderness, Alessandro had prepared for Ramona a bed of finely broken twigs of the manzanita and ceanothus. . . . Above these he spread layers of glossy ferns, five and six feet long." Ramona laid down to rest. Alessandro made no bed for himself. He was to watch the night through, that no harm should come to his Majella. "Ramona was very tired and she was very happy. All night long she slept like a child. She did not hear Alessandro's steps. . . . Hour after hour Alessandro sat leaning against a huge sycamore trunk, and watched her. . . . She looked like a saint, he thought." The artist fully grasped this sweet and peaceful scene. He made the canvas record and retell the implicit trust of Ramona, the gallant chivalry of Alessandro.

In the graveyard at Temecula Alessandro and Ramona met Carmena, an Indian woman, crazed with grief, who was passing her days at her baby's grave in Pachanga and her nights by her husband's at Temecula; all the result of American aggression in the Indians' country. Carmena watched with Ramona while Alessandro went to Hartsel's in Temecula to secure his father's violin. The reproduction of this incident on canvas by Mr. Sandham is in illustration of the lines of the story reading: "Dismounting, and taking Baba's bridle over her arm, she bowed her head assentingly, and still keeping firm hold of Carmena's hand, followed her." It is a touching scene, and a test of the artistic ability of the painter.

The day after their marriage Alessandro and Ramona arrived at San Pasquale, where had located some of Alessandro's Temecula people, who wondered "how it had come about that she, so beautiful, and nurtured in the Moreno house, of which they all knew, should be Alessandro's loving wife. . . . Toward night they came, bringing in a hand-barrow the most aged woman in the village, to look at her. She wished to see the beautiful stranger. . . . Those who had borne her withdrew and seated themselves a few paces off. Alessandro spoke first. In a few words he told the old woman of Ramona's birth, of their marriage, and of her new name of adoption." Then followed words from Ramona, interpreted by Alessandro; and the old woman, lifting up her arms like a sibyl, said: "It is well; I am your mother. The winds of the valley shall love you, and the grass shall dance when you come." The painting of Mr. Sandham shows the old woman and other Indians seated, Ramona kneeling and Alessandro standing, bending, with his left hand on Ramona's right shoulder. It presents an affecting climax, and evidences the genius of the artist.

When Felipe, in his first search for Ramona and Alessandro, arrived at Santa Barbara Mission, "the first figure he saw was the venerable Father Salvierderra sitting in the corridor. As Felipe approached, the old man's face beamed with pleasure, and he came forward tottering, leaning on a staff in each hand. 'Welcome, my son,' was the Father's greeting, and he asked, 'Are all well?' Felipe knew then the Father had not seen Ramona, and dismay seized him. And when Felipe told him he was seeking Ramona, the Father cried, 'Ramona! . . . Seeking Ramona! What has befallen the blessed child?'" The painting is emotional and enlivens the text of the story to action.

The portrait of Felipe, the eldest son of Señora Moreno, presents a Mexican gentleman of culture and character. The sombrero and cigarette of the Mexican are in evidence. Instead of a front there is a side view of the subject. The picture is an interesting study of a young man who adored and wished to please his mother, who loved Ramona ardently, but rationally and unselfishly, and who was scorched by the fire that raged between the cold and haughty Señora and the lovable and innocent Ramona; and who, at the end of the tragedy, sought Ramona, discovered her as Alessandro's widow, took her and her child to Camulos, and afterward went with them to Mexico City, where the two were married. "Sons and daughters came to bear his name. The daughters were all beautiful; but the most beautiful of them all, and, it was said, the most beloved by both father and mother, was the oldest one; the one who bore the mother's name, and was only stepdaughter to the Señor —Ramona—Ramona, daughter of Alessandro, the Indian."

The canvas story of the brutal and tragic murder of Alessandro by Jim Farrar is a painting of distressing horror. It shows Jim Farrar on horseback and Alessandro stepping out of his dwelling, his hands pleadingly lifted, Ramona leaning against the open door, her hands to her face, the picture of grief and despair. Capitan, the faithful collie, is at Ramona's side. The painting is true to the story of Alessandro's death.

The decorative chapter headings from Mr. Sandham's sketches are an interesting feature of the illustrated edition of "Ramona." They have for their subjects the Camulos chapel, the torn altar cloth, different Mission buildings, Indian baskets, Temecula village, Mission bells, and other objects described in "Ramona." All these sketches are faithfully correct.

The portrait of Father Salvierderra painted for the "Pasadena Edition" of "Ramona," is not to be confused with the original portrait of that character produced by Mr. Sandham from life while he was at Santa Barbara with Mrs. Jackson in 1883. Of this original portrait Mr. Sandham's daughter, Miss Gwendoline Sandham, residing in London, has thus written the authors: "It is a very fine water-color, and perhaps the best picture my father ever painted, and has been 'hung on the line' in most of the world's big exhibitions; and though, for form's sake, it has been catalogued with a price, it has always been exhibited with the red star, 'sold,' on it, as it was my mother's property. It is now mine. It is a portrait study of the original of Father Salvierderra, and was painted, I believe, in the cloister of Santa Barbara Mission."

When Mr. Sandham was making the "Ramona" sketches at Santa Barbara Mission, including the original portrait of Father Salvierderra, the prototype of this character, Father Sanchez, gave to the artist his cassock,

PORTRAIT OF FATHER SALVIERDERRA

From the original portrait of Father Salvierderra, painted from life by Mr Henry Sandham, the artist of "Ramona," in the cloister at Santa Barbara Mission, 1883. The bell is the "Death Bell," at Santa Barbara Mission. *Page 144.* (*Permission of Miss Gwendoline Sandham, London.*)

HOME OF TEMECULA INDIANS AND SAN DIEGO MISSION

(1) The home of Temecula Indians, who, having been driven from that village by the whites, took up their abode at Pechanga, three miles away Mrs. Jackson passed a night in this Indian abode. (2) Interior of chapel at San Diego Mission, where Alessandro and Ramona were married. "In a neglected weedy open stood his (Father Gaspara's) chapel, * * * the most profoundly melancholy in all Southern California." "*Ramona.*"

cowl, sandals and the hempen girdle with its symbolical five knots. The sandals were well worn, and, to quote from Mr. Sandham's note to the "Pasadena Edition" of "Ramona," "the cowl bleached and faded with the sun—marks of the endless round of toils and duties so faithfully described by Mrs. Jackson."

From a letter received from Miss Gwendoline Sandham by the authors the following is of special interest: "It might interest you to know that the Franciscan robe my father mentions in his little note to 'Ramona,' is still in my possession. The father gave it to him himself on the condition that it should never be used for masquerading, theatrical displays, etc. Unfortunately the sandals and girdle are missing, and I fear the moths have played sad havoc with the robe itself, but it is a very real memento of the original of Father Salvierderra, and as such my father always held it in sacred regard. If you care to have the remains of the robe to be presented to the City of Los Angeles I will be very glad to send it on to you."

The authors have accepted the offer of Miss Sandham, and the robe of Father Salvierderra will be disposed of in due time as directed by her.

That Mr. Sandham was an artist of great

versatility is evidenced alone by the variety of subjects of the "Ramona" illustrations. His portrait of Father Salvierderra would be a credit to Van Dyck; the scene of demonstrative love between Alessandro and Ramona on horseback proves him an animal painter of the talent of Landseer; his Mission buildings and landscapes are worthy of Fortuny.

It should be gratifying to "Ramona" lovers in California to know that the original paintings of Mr. Sandham, from which were taken the illustrations of the "Pasadena Edition" of "Ramona," are in California, having been purchased and being now owned by Mr. C. C. Parker of Los Angeles, a book-dealer and a book-lover, who pays tribute always to Helen Hunt Jackson and lauds the artistic genius of Henry Sandham.

The wide range of Mr. Sandham's talent was beyond the ordinary. It would be difficult to name an artist who sketched and painted so many and such a variety of subjects as did he. He was equally brilliant with animate and inanimate things; portraits, landscapes, buildings, animals and character scenes and studies.

"The Battle of Lexington," bought by public subscription, which now hangs in the city hall at Lexington, is his work. His picture of two moose in a death struggle was awarded a gold medal at the Paris Exhibition. In Canada his best known canvas is his portrait of Sir John Macdonald, at Ottawa, which the latter's widow has declared to be the "most speaking likeness" ever painted of Canada's greatest statesman.

The Canadian Government purchased and has at Ottawa several other of his paintings, the best being "St. Mark's of Venice."

There was a Memorial Exhibition of Mr. Sandham's sketches and paintings, found in his studio after his death, at the Imperial Institute, London, under the patronage of all the former living Governors General of Canada, and the then recently appointed one, H. R. H., the Duke of Connaught; and other prominent persons, including United States Ambassador, Hon. Whitelaw Reid. One gallery was reserved entirely for the royal reception. Four hundred and sixty-six pictures and sketches of the dead artist were exhibited. In the list were these California subjects: "Death Bell of the Brothers," Santa Barbara Mission; portrait, "Father Salvierderra"; "California Hydraulic Mining"; "Young Chinese Merchant"; "On a California Ranch"; "After Sundown"; "The Priests' Garden," Santa Barbara Mission; "Cactus in Bloom"; "Mountain Clouds"; "California."

During most of the time Mr. Sandham was in Los Angeles he made his home at the hacienda of Don Antonio and Doña Mariana de Coronel. Mrs. Jackson introduced him to this courteous and hospitable couple, and asked as a favor that he be permitted to be in their home, so, as Mrs. Jackson stated, he might hear stories of the Mission Indians and study and sketch them in life. She especially requested that the Coronels should select Indians as subjects for Mr. Sandham's work.

For two months at a time Mr. Sandham was at the Coronel home, working earnestly and constantly. His illustrations of Mrs. Jackson's writings were but a minor part of his drawings and paintings while in California. "He was an enthusiastic worker," said Doña Mariana de Coronel to the authors. "I have known him to sketch and paint from four to five subjects in one day, all complete. My husband and I brought to him many Indians, men, women and children, dressed in their native costumes, and assisted in posing them for Mr. Sandham, who sketched and painted them. He was a most courteous and considerate gentleman. Whenever any person or thing attracted him, out came his pencil and sketch-book and he earnestly proceeded to work. I remember well one day I was returning to the kitchen from the orchard, carrying a panful of freshly picked peaches. He saw me, and I had to please him by stopping until he sketched me. He said he wanted the picture to send to his wife. Mrs. Jackson and Mr. Sandham were congenial and harmonious companions. Both were enthusiastic in their respective lines of labor."

From a source other than Señora de Coronel the authors have the information that Mr. Sandham pronounced her the best and nearest type of the Madonna he had ever seen in life. He painted a bust picture of her, which he kept in a prominent place in his eastern studio, which he always designated as "My California Madonna."

Mr. Sandham's description of an evening at the Coronel home is interesting, and evidences the pleasure of his stay there, and is here given:

"We were sitting on the veranda, whence we could count thirty different kinds of roses, and Don Antonio in the gentle Spanish was telling us of the California of the past. Señora, his charming young wife, interpreted for us, often beginning a sentence before he had quite finished, their voices unconsciously blending in one harmonious chord, to which Don Antonio, leaning back, dressed in full Mexican costume, kept up a gentle accompaniment on the guitar. The various ranch hands, sauntering up, seated themselves in a semicircle at the foot of the stairs, a picturesque group in their broad-brimmed sombreros with serapes draped about their shoulders. In the deepening darkness the only lights came from the cigarettes of the men, whose interest, like our own, was concentrated on the recital of the Don. There, with music and the scent of roses filling the night, we lingered, to listen to stories of the forgotten past, and to learn of old customs of the California that was. It was here that we learned for the first time of the singing of the sunrise hymn so artistically introduced in Chapters V and XI of 'Ramona.'"

After witnessing the shearing of a band of sheep at "Lucky" Baldwin's ranch, Mrs. Jackson sat in an unusually prolonged silence. It was Mr. Sandham who said to her, "You are tired?"; to which she thoughtfully and feelingly answered: "No; but for the first time in my life I appreciate the scriptural text, 'As a sheep before her shearers is dumb.'" "The helpless protest of the Mission Indians," wrote

THE GRAPE ARBOR, CAMULOS, LEADING TO THE WILLOWS AT THE WASHING STONES

"A wide sidewalk, shaded by a trellis, * * * knotted and twisted with grapevines, lead straight down * * * to a little brook at the foot of it." "*Ramona.*"

THE GUITAR AND "THE DEATH BELL"

(1) The guitar of Don Antonio de Coronel, brought to California in 1835, with which he frequently entertained Helen Hunt Jackson. Now in the Coronel Collection, Chamber of Commerce, Los Angeles. "Don Antonio * * * dressed in full Mexican garb, kept up a gentle accompaniment on the guitar" *Page 254.*
(2) "The Death Bell," Santa Barbara Mission, made in 1737 "On the corridor of the inner court hangs a bell which is rung for the hours of the daily offices and secular duties. It is also struck whenever a friar dies, to announce that all is over It is the duty of the brother who has watched the last breath of the dying one to go immediately and strike this bell. Its sad note has echoed many times through the corridor" (Mrs. Jackson in "*Glimpses of California and the Missions.*")

Mr. Sandham, "had a new meaning for her from that moment."

Henry Sandham's work is inseparably connected with "Ramona." In conversing with him concerning the novel Mrs. Jackson was wont to designate it as "our book."

The original paintings from which the illustrations of the novel were taken should belong to the public, and to this end the authors are negotiating with the owner, that they may be placed for all time in the Los Angeles Museum of History, Science and Art. They do mute but just tribute to Henry Sandham, companion and co-worker in California with Helen Hunt Jackson.

"His pieces so with live objects strive,
That both or pictures seem, or both alive,
Nature herself, amaz'd, does doubting stand,
Which is her own and which the painter's hand;
And does attempt the like with less success,
When her own work in twins she would express.
His all-resembling pencil did out-pass
The mimic imagery of looking-glass.
Nor was his life less perfect than his art,
Nor was his hand less erring than his heart,
There was no false or fading color there,
The figures sweet and full proportioned were."

CHAPTER XIX

THE DRAMATIZATION OF "RAMONA"

IT is among the strangest anomalies of histrionic annals in the United States that the great American novel should never have been successfully dramatized. There would seem to be in the romance of Mrs. Jackson a superabundance of genuine dramatic material, a plethora of tragic as well as dramatic incidents, any amount of sentiment and pathos, with opportunities for the introduction of folklore and folk-song almost boundless, with the widest range for the costuming of characters and the introduction of stage effects. Yet fifty-three distinct failures to dramatize the story have been recorded, while "Uncle Tom's Cabin" holds the record for the largest aggregate box sales of any American play ever staged.

What more beautiful characters than those of Ramona and Alessandro? What more sublime character than that of Father Salvierderra? Where will be found such genuine spiritual devotion as is shown in all the members of Señora Moreno's household? Where such another exhibition of true maidenly love as that of Ramona for Alessandro? Where a more chivalrous lover than Alessandro? Where such an incident of pure, patient devotion as that of Felipe for the girl his mother could not love? What play-writer could ask for greater emotional climaxes than the discovery by the Indian of the wondrous beauty of the maiden, and the joyful hint that the blood of his race ran in her veins? Or the unfortunate discovery by Señora Moreno of the two at the first love-making in the willows? What more thrilling scene than the fainting of Felipe on the wool-shed and the night flight of José to Temecula for the violin?

What prettier setting than the meeting of Father Salvierderra with Ramona in the mustard field? What more sisterly devotion and innocent conception than that displayed by Ramona in saving Margarita from disgrace and punishment for carelessness in handling the altar cloth? What more pathetic scene than the deathbed of Señora Moreno, pointing her bony finger at the hidden chamber, wherein the Ramona jewels were kept, and struggling for breath to articulate the secret she had so long kept from her son? What more terrible scene than the driving of the Indians from their homes at Temecula at the point of the bayonet? What more thrilling tragedy than the slaying of Alessandro before the very eyes of his devoted Majella? What more romantic spectacle than the night journeys over the mountains to San Diego of the homeless lovers, the devotion of the one, the perfect trustfulness of the other? Where could be found another such wholesome, genuinely good soul as Aunt Ri?

The story is clean, instructive and uplifting throughout, the purpose sublime, the end sad but sweet.

And yet it never has been successfully dramatized or staged. The last unfortunate and inexplicable failure, too, occurred in the very heart of Ramonaland, where local color was in the very atmosphere, and every heart in the audience pulsated with fervid sympathy with the theme.

Passing strange, but all too true. It was at the Mason Opera House, Los Angeles. Never a larger or more enthusiastic audience. Never a more fashionable or aristocratic one. Never an audience more kind or patient or considerate; yet never one so disappointed. Ramona was "played" till twelve o'clock, and the people went to their homes grieving as one might over the fall and breakage of a beautiful vase. The writer grieved with the rest, sorry for the dramatist, sorry for the actors and actresses, yet more filled with compassion for the audience.

Some day a real dramatist will rise up and give to the American people a correct presentation of one of the sweetest, most pathetic and soulful stories ever written.

HELEN HUNT JACKSON *

Ina Coolbrith

What songs found voice upon those lips,
  What magic dwelt within the pen,
Whose music into silence slips,
  Whose spell lives not again!

For her the clamorous to-day
  The dreamful yesterday became;
The brands upon dead hearths that lay
  Leaped into living flame.

Clear ring the silvery Mission bells
  Their calls to vesper and to mass;
O'er vineyard slopes, thro' fruited dells,
  The long processions pass.

The pale Franciscan lifts in air
  The cross above the kneeling throng;
Their simple world how sweet with prayer,
  With chant and matin song!

There, with her dimpled, lifted hands,
  Parting the mustard's golden plumes,
The dusky maid, Ramona, stands,
  Amid the sea of blooms.

* From "Songs from the Golden Gate," with permission.

And Alessandro, type of all
  His broken tribe, for evermore
An exile, hears the stranger call
  Within his father's door.

The visions vanish and are not,
  Still are the sounds of peace and strife,
Passed with the earnest heart and thought
  Which lured them back to life.

O, sunset land! O, land of vine,
  And rose, and bay! in silence here
Let fall one little leaf of thine,
  With love, upon her bier.

GLOSSARY OF SPANISH WORDS

Alejandro	Ä-lā-hän′-drō
Alessandro	Ä-lās-sän′-drō
Avila	Ä′-vē-lä
Blanca Yndart	Blän′-cä Ē̄n-där′t
Cahuilla	Kä-hwē′-lyä
Camulos	Kä-mōō′-lōs
Canero	Kä-nā′-rō
Canito	Kä-nē′-tō
Cilicio	Thē-lē′-thē-ō
Conejos	Kō-nā′-hōs
Corralez (Corrales)	Kōr-rä-lāth′ (Cor-ra′l-es)
Del Valle	Dāl Vä′-lyā
Domingo García	Dō-mē′n-gō Gär-thē′-ä
Don	Dōn
Doña	Dō′-nyä
El Recreo	Āl Rā-crā′-ō
El Retrio	Āl Rā-trē′-ō
Felipe	Fā-lē′-pā
Francisco de Jesús Sańchez	Frän-thē′s-cō dā Hā-sōō′s Sä′n-chāth
Frijoles	Frē-hō′-lās
Gonzaga	Gōn-thä′-gä
Grevoja Pa	Grā-vō′-hä Pä
Guadalajara	Gwä-dä-lä-hä′-rä
Guadalupe	Gwä-dä-lōō′-pā
Guajome	Gwä-hō′-mā
Guanajuato	Gwä-nä-hwä′-tō
Hacienda	Ä-thēān′-dä
Hispano	Ē̄-spä′-nō
Ignacio	Ē̄g-nä′-thē-ō
Inez	Ē̄-nā′th
Joaquin	Hwä-kēē′n

GLOSSARY OF SPANISH WORDS

José	Hō-sā′
José Jesús López	Hō-sā′ Hā-sōō′s Lō′-pāth
José Pachito	Hō-sā′ Pä-chē′-tō
Josefa	Hō-sā′-fä
Juan	Hwän
Juanita	Hwä-nē′-tä
Junipero Serra	Hōō-nē′-pā-rō Sā′r-rä
La Jolla (La Joya)	Lä Hō′-lyä (Lä Hō′-yä)
Lä Puente	Lä Pōō-ān′-tā
Lequan	Lā′-kwän
Los Angeles	Lōs Än′-hā-lās
Los Coyotes	Lōs Kō-yō′-tās
Majel	Mä-hāl′
Majella	Mä-hā′-lyä
Mesa Grande	Mā′-sä Grä′n-dā
Moreno	Mō-rā′-nō
Mortero	Mōr-tā′-rō
Nacha	Nä′-chä
Nachita	Nä-chē′-tä
Navacana	Nä-vä-kä′-nä
Pablo Assis	Pä′-blō Äs-sē′s
Padre	Pä′-drā
Pájaro	Pä′-hä-rō
Pala	Pä′-lä
Peyri	Pā′y-rē
Pío Pico	Pē′-ō Pē′-cō
Pirú	Pē-rōō′
Potrero	Pō-trā′-rō
Ramona	Rä-mō′-nä
Rancherias	Rän-chā-rē′-äs
Rancho	Rä′n-chō
Rivero	Rē-vā′-rō
Rojerio Rocha	Rō-hā′-rē-ō Rō′-chä
Salvierderra	Säl-vē-ār-dā′r-rä
San Blas	Sän Bläs
San Corgonio	Sän Cōr-gō′-nē-ō
San Jacinto	Sän Hä-thēn′-tō

San Luis Obispo	Sän Lōō'-ēs O-bē's-pō
San Luis Rey	Sän Lōō'-ēs Rāy
San Ysidro	Sän Ē-sē'-drō
Santa Ynez	Sä'n-tä Ē-nā'th
Señor	Sā-nyō'r
Señora	Sā-nyō'-rä
Serapes	Sā-rä'-pās
Tehachapi	Tā-ä-chä'-pē
Ulpiano	Ōōl-pēä'-nō
Vaquero	Vä-kā'-rō
Varela	Vä-rā'-lä
Vibiana	Vē-bēä'-nä
Ybare (Ybarra)	Ē-bä'r-rā (Ē-bä'r-rä)
Ygnacio	Ēg-nä'-thē-ō
Yndart	Ēn-dä'rt
Ysabel	Ē-sä-bā'l
Zacatecas	Thä-kä-tā'-käs
Zalvidea	Thäl-vē'-dā-ä

www.ingramcontent.com/pod-product-compliance
Lightning Source LLC
LaVergne TN
LVHW011159110826
845150LV00006B/1267